Million Dollar Agent

Brokering the Dream

Million Dollar Agent

Brokering the Dream

Josh Flagg

polimedia
publishing

All Polimedia Publishing titles, imprints, and distributed lines are available at special quantity discounts for bulk purchases for sales promotion, premiums, fundraising, educational, or institutional use.

Special book excerpts or customized printings can also be created to fit specific needs. For details, write or contact the office of Polimedia Publishing at:

Polimedia Publishers
440 S. El Cielo Road, #3-670
Palm Springs, CA 92262
info@polimediaent.com
www.polimediaent.com

3 4 5 6 7 8 9 10

Published by Polimedia Publishers
© 2011 Josh Flagg

ISBN-13: 978-0-9768617-9-9

Printed in the United States of America

To Mom, Dad, Colton and Grandma Edith.
Thank you for your patience... lots of patience!

Table of Contents

Preface

Before you criticize someone, you should walk a mile in their shoes. That way, when you criticize them, you're a mile away and you have their shoes. -- Jack Hadley

I told Steve, a friend of mine, that I was going to write my autobiography. I said to him, "Do you think I am too young to do this, Steve?"

He said, "No one could be more prepared than you."

So, I began to weigh the pros and cons of putting my life onto paper. I concluded that if I did record my life, then died immediately afterward, at least people would know the real me. On the other hand, if I lived another fifty or sixty years, I may really have screwed myself. I decided to write it anyway.

I was advised by many people including my friends, my family – nearly everyone whoever came within five inches of me – to leave certain aspects of my life out of the book, the bulk of it, in fact. I was unsure how to feel about this advice until I remembered a quote by Oscar Wilde, "Biography lends to death a new terror." Once you are dead, people often feel free to say what they like about you - whether true or false- because you aren't around to dispute them. I don't really fear what others may say about me once I'm gone. Nevertheless, I would rather set the record straight while I am still here.

I cannot help the fact that people have talked about me my entire life. More often behind my back than to my face, sad proof there are few gentlemen left in this world, but what can you do? And, what of those who say hurtful things, there are plenty of other people with kind things to say. Perhaps not as many of them, but they are around! Do I mind being talked about? You bet I don't! Better to be talked about than not be noticed at all, after all, who wants to go unnoticed?

It's true there are many people who have not liked me, but that is only because I was always so different from everyone else. I have never fit in easily, and that is probably why I am always attracted to unique, unconventional people. As I mentioned, I have always been different. Even as a child, I never heard the same drumbeat everyone else seemed to hear.

If you want to know exactly when I decided to write my book, it was on February 10th, 2010. I was in my grandmother's suite at the Carlyle in New York City, watching a CNN news program. The reporter was doing a story on Tahiti, and a bell suddenly went off in my head. "Tahiti, Tahiti," I thought, "What do I have to do with Tahiti?" Isn't that one of the many places I have been privileged enough to visit? And then I remembered, five years earlier I had flown to Tahiti. I was there to photograph a nearby private island I was selling at the time. I had actually made the eighteen-hour flight, stayed for one night, then turned right around to come home. As I lay on the sofa, I found myself thinking how strange a thing that was to have done.

I began to recollect other occasions when I'd done equally crazy things, such as fly clients around Beverly Hills in helicopters or wrap houses in big red bows, and it didn't take long to realize that all of these experiences could add up to one fascinating book. I began jotting them down, along with anything and everything else I recalled of my past.

At first, I worried that twenty-five years might be too short a lifetime to warrant a book. I was unsure how to keep the story of my short life interesting. Would I have to add 'fluff' to my story, or tell my life as I wished it had happened? In doing either, I would turn my book into a work of fiction, something I didn't want to do. I wanted the story I told to be the unvarnished truth, to answer questions about me, not just for others, but for myself as well. And that is how this book came to be.

Those of you who think you know me well, you had better prepare yourselves for a surprise. You don't know a quarter of who I really am. I happen to be a pretty private person, one who doesn't easily open up about my emotions or my personal life. For those of you I haven't met, I hope the tale of my life, both the good and the bad, will be as entertaining for you as it has been for me. I've experienced many, many wonderful things, and many horrible things, but I've also accumulated a heck of a lot of fun memories along the way.

So here it is, the truth, the whole truth and nothing but the truth. I hope you enjoy this for what it is, merely a loosely organized recollection of my memories, be it funny or sad, or both. Thank you for making me part of your life.

On a final note, this is not just an autobiography. This book encompasses my knowledge of the city of Los Angeles, of the people and the culture, the great estates of Beverly Hills and the Golden Age of Hollywood. This book is mostly though, my attempt to convey to the reader my best advice on how to become a successful real estate agent. Now, enjoy. You better... there are no refunds!

The Formative Years

It was a Monday morning, the year 1988. My mother and I were traveling in her sleek black convertible turning right onto the world famous Sunset Strip from Doheny Drive north of Sunset. I remember the turn as if it were yesterday. I can still smell the camel colored leather of her car, forever wafting through my memory. I don't think my mother ever once had the convertible top down. I used to frequently ask her, "Mom, why do you buy convertibles if you don't put the top down, we live in one of the best climates in the country?" Her reply, "Because I don't want to get skin cancer." Oh brother! But my life did not start in 1988. This is simply the first thing I can remember.

I was born on August 20th, 1985, and not at Cedars-Sinai Hospital as many Jewish children are, but at St. John's Hospital, a Catholic Hospital near the ocean. We did not live anywhere near St. John's but my mother liked a particular obstetrician there, and she was willing to make the journey every week to ensure the very best for her baby.

At around 4:00AM, after several hours of difficult labor, a baby boy slowly emerged. My mother cried with joy, my father fainted. I'm told she immediately changed from the hospital gown, into a colorful Emilio Pucci negligee. It was clearly a sign, no not that I was gay, but that everything from that point forward in my life would always be different. I would not face the world with my mom dressed in a drab hospital gown, no, I had to come in with a bang, and I would live life that way as well.

The first indication that I had a fascination with fancy homes and buildings, started when I was three years old. I built an entire city out of wooden blocks and Legos, which covered half of the floor of my bedroom. I would not let anyone touch or get near "the city," and as I grew, so did "the city." It was not until I was seven or eight years old that I begrudgingly disassembled "the city" and removed it from my bedroom floor. This was a great relief to our housekeeper, as she was not allowed to vacuum in that section for fear of knocking something over, and thus, having to bear witness to my evil wrath.

Now, that first morning in 1988, after we turned the corner onto Sunset Boulevard, I remember my mother saying to me, "Honey this is your first day of nursery school and now you are a big boy!" I remember thinking to myself, "I am three-years-old, how big could I possibly be, I wonder if I will remember this moment ten years from now?"

I went to a little nursery school on Santa Monica Boulevard called the Creative Center. My mom sent me there because my older sister Dana had attended nine years before. That first morning my mother pulled into the driveway of the school, she unbuckled me from my car seat and led me through the big blue door. I remember that the door handle was at the very top, so children could not escape this prison -like compound.

I could see that there were a bunch of children sitting at tables entertaining themselves with play dough and I remember thinking to myself, "This doesn't look too stimulating." So it was then that I had my very first of many temper tantrums to come. It would mark the beginning of years of screaming and crying until I got what I wanted. I started to erupt and the tears streamed down my face. I remember a large busted teacher pinning me down as my mother attempted to leave. I did not want my mother to go. It was the first time in my life being away from my mom.

I thought to myself, "Maybe if I calm down, and pretend to have lost interest in her, I can outwit this teacher into letting me go, and then I can make a quick run back into my mother's arms." It worked, the woman released me and I stood there for a few seconds just to affirm that everything was okay. As she turned her body, I suddenly made a run for it, and I ran as fast as I could. I ran down the corridor and into the reception of the nursery school. My mother was already half way out the blue door on her way to getting back into her car. As I ran harder and harder, trying to escape from that horrible place, and the big breasted woman, I finally approached the blue door, but alas, the handle was too high for me to reach. I looked out the window and watched my mother's car pulling away. She drove off, smoke billowing out her tailpipe, the letters 'SL' getting smaller in the distance. I realized then and there that in life you don't always get your way, but I wasn't about to give up without a fight.

After a few weeks at the Creative Center, I realized this place wasn't so bad after all, and in fact I kind of liked it. There were arts and crafts, a sandbox and of course, dress up! I definitely didn't know I would swing the other way at the time, but looking back on it now, I recall having an innate fondness for a boy my age named Jonah. I don't know where he is today. He probably has a girlfriend, maybe he's even married, but I guess you could say he was the first boy I ever took an interest in.

One afternoon, as my mother was picking me up from school, she strapped me into the car and gave me my Minute Maid apple juice box drink. Within seconds it was on the floor, spilling everywhere and soaking into the carpet. As she stepped out of the car to throw the juice box into the alley dumpster, I thought,

3

"This would be a great time to learn how to drive," and began to shift myself into the driver's seat.

At that moment, a young boy from Israel named Ari was walking behind the car with his nanny. I yelled out the window, "Ari, look... I can drive! I am driving!" I don't know if I was more interested in impressing him with my driving skills, or that my first car was a Mercedes convertible. Knowing myself, probably the latter.

As it was, my mother had parked on the school driveway, which was on a bit of a slope, and as I released the hand brake to put the car into gear, the car began to roll backwards. Ari, I could tell, was impressed. So much so, that as the car began to roll, he just stood there, behind the car, and continued to stand there, as it continued rolling backwards. The car literally came within inches of rolling over him, when his nanny, probably more interested in saving her job than the boy's own life, darted into action and pushed him out of the way. Thankfully, my mom had seen what had happened and ran from the dumpster in time to apply the hand brake before any more harm could occur. This wouldn't be the last time though that I decided to take the car out for a spin, but more on that later.

Ever since I was a little boy, I've had a weird obsession with keys, and not just car keys, but house keys as well. At family functions, or at any event when I was around a lot of people, my father would tell everyone ahead of time to hide their keys because I would somehow find a way into their pockets, take their keys and visit them at their homes in the middle of the night. Needless to say, I remember one particular Thanksgiving when I had disappeared and everyone started looking for me. Then all of a sudden, a light bulb went off in my father's head, and my parents found me, car keys in my hand, sleeping in my uncle Len and

4

Aunt Nancy's garage. Keys to me represented freedom, and quite possibly the purchase of my first home.

5

North Doheny

I was very fortunate to grow up in one of the nicest parts of Los Angeles. We lived a block north of Sunset Boulevard, off of Doheny Drive, in an area that is one of the hottest locations to buy a property. When I was young, people moved there because they wanted the location of Beverly Hills (just one and a half blocks West), but without the pretentiousness and the snobbishness that the name carries.

Many people think that because these properties don't have the 90210 zip code, that they must not carry as high of a price tag. Truth-in-fact, a home off or on Doheny Drive north of Sunset, will always command a higher price per-square-foot than a home within the 90210 zip code. Entertainment icons such as Keanu Reeves, Leonardo DiCaprio, Halle Berry, Jodie Foster, Tobey Maguire, Jennifer Anniston, David Arquette, Courtney Cox, Michael and Pat York, Cheryl Ladd, Megan Mullally, Tyler Perry, Herbie Hancock, Dionne Warwick, Jerry Herman, Ricardo Montalban, James Cagney, George Harrison, John Lennon, Madonna, President Reagan, Christina Aguilera, Diana Ross, David Geffen and legendary film director George Cukor, have all at one time or another called this hill their home.

Wondering if big families with noisy kids would live there? Unlikely. Many of the homes are perched on the edge of a hill with a fifty-foot drop below. Many of these multi-million dollar properties don't even really have backyards. People pay the big bucks for these homes because of the privacy and the view. My parents were lucky that they purchased a home that has a great backyard, a view, and wonderful privacy. When I was growing up, even with all of the celebrities that lived there, the neighborhood was so quiet and low-key. Now when you come out of your front door, at any hour of the day, you will see busses driving by filled with tourists staring at their maps to the stars' homes.

When I was younger, my friends would ask me, "Where do you live? What do you call that area?" At the time I didn't have the slightest idea and I would say, "Well it's not exactly Beverly Hills, and it's not exactly the Hollywood Hills." I have heard it referred to as the Sunset Strip, but it's more like the Malibu of the Westside; overpriced, very eclectic in the style of houses, and a Range Rover, Ferrari or Jag in every single driveway. The Hill is where I first became interested in real estate. My father would drive me through the neighborhood, up and around the streets surrounding our home, and together we would look at open houses, not because we wanted to move, but simply because it was fun.

At sixteen, when I got my driver's license, it was the biggest sense of freedom I could imagine. I had been living in a fish bowl, just waiting to get out and explore my surroundings. For a young man with a fascination for beautiful and expensive homes, being able to pull out of my parents driveway that day, and go wherever I wanted to go, was completely exhilarating.

Where did I go first? You are probably thinking I drove over to a friend's house like most kids do when they first get their license. No, not at all. I actually took the entire afternoon and drove up and down the neighborhood, one street at a time, to explore every nook and cranny of that hill. You see, I did not care to share that moment with friends. This was my moment, and I was mesmerized.

The Flagg Residence

I only slept in a crib for the first nine months of my life. One evening, I guess I had decided that I had had enough of those cramped quarters and I climbed out of my crib. In the morning, my parents found to their dismay, a grinning little boy in bed with them. They tried to keep me in my crib, but night after night I would reappear in their bed until finally they realized that my sleeping in a crib wasn't going to work.

So they let me stay in their bedroom, well actually, I slept in their walk-in closet. I could have slept right by their bed, but I just felt more comfortable in the closet (should have figured.) Maybe because I liked playing with my mother's purses and heels, maybe because there was excellent lighting and lots of mirrors. I don't know what it was, but I really enjoyed it in there and it felt very natural to me. My mom, around one o' clock every morning, would take me out of the closet and walk me to my bedroom where I would finish out the night in my own room. It took me until I was six-years-old before I could finally fall asleep in my own bedroom.

From the time I was born until I was around ten-years-old, my parents went through a slew of housekeepers and nannies. None of them could tolerate me though. My parents could not hold onto any of them no matter what they did, and by the time I was ten, we had gone through more housekeepers than you have fingers. There was the screamer Xiomara, whom my mother fired on the spot when she heard her ranting one day. There was Diane, who made us call her Iahaa until we finally found out that Iahaa meant servant in her native language. There was Andrea, the one who liked to suck on my toes, and then there was Helga, the one who had a fondness for giving me bubble baths....with her in them. Three Connie's, two Lillie's and ten housekeepers later, we finally found Silvia, who still works for my parents today.

Of my sister Dana, I have many memories of us growing up, although I must admit they are mostly of us fighting. Regardless of our childhood bickering, she is my big sister and I love her even though I avoid reminding her. Dana is not my father's daughter by blood, but he still raised both of us equally, well actually truth be told, I think he favored Dana. Dana and my dad may have had a better relationship growing up, but it did not bother me too much because I had other things on my mind, like floral arrangements, toile window coverings and thread counts.

My parents were and are, very low-key people. I grew up in a very nice house, in a very expensive area, but nothing over the top and nothing super flashy. Anyone who came to our house could tell we had money just by looking at the art on our walls, but having "the big flashy house in Bel Air," was not my parents' style. In fact, it was everything they did not want.

My parents did not need a $12,000,000.00 home in Holmby Hills. They are much more comfortable in a beautiful 4,500 square-foot home on the hill. I think my parents would be happy living on a ranch in the middle of the country as long as they had each other. They have never been impressed by who has what, and how many square feet they have. They just like to have fun and the rest of that "stuff" is unimportant to them.

As low-key and unpretentious as my parents are, and despite my mother always saying to me, "I don't know where you came from, how are you my child?" I blame them both for my precocious demeanor and pretentious sense of self-worth. My reasoning for this is that my parents exposed me to things that most other children not only were not exposed to, but also really have no interest in. My mother as a young girl, and my father later in life were, simply put, exposed to really nice "things." During my childhood those "things" just happened to be hanging on our walls or casually exhibited on our tables.

My father grew up in a home of European Jewish immigrants. When they first came to this country they had very little money and it was not until later in life that they became well off. As a result, my father was not spoiled as a child. He had to work for anything and everything. When he was younger, getting baked beans on the table was a treat for him. My father tried to instill the same values in me, but in doing so never realized that this was not 1950 and he could not expect the same from his son that his father expected from him nearly forty years earlier. I don't need to tell you, it was rough growing up when every time I had something nice or I did something nice for myself, my dad made me feel like I was in the 1920's depression-era. I don't know how I would have survived without my mom constantly telling him, "Stop treating Josh like we were in Nazi-occupied Europe."

So you see growing up for me was very strange. Even though I admit I did have the life sized stuffed animals, the electric cars and the antique doll house (don't ask,) I somehow felt badly about these things because of my dad's attitude of not wanting me to be spoiled. This had a big impact on me then, and even a greater impact on me later in life. It caused years of conflicted feelings. Having nice things but being told by my dad that I shouldn't take them for granted. My childhood was a mixture of many different emotions. However, one thing is certain, my parents were fabulous parents; I just was not able to understand my dad's philosophy. Now I understand what he was doing, he was trying to instill

13

values in me. But unfortunately he took it too far and gave me a sense of insecurity, which still exists in me today. In doing so, I retaliated and showed him that I didn't care, I was entitled, and I would do whatever the hell I wanted.

In other words, his plan to make me a humble human being backfired. At the same time, I feel badly for my dad. If his shoes were not clean as a child, his father would throw them away as a form of punishment. It was hard for my dad to part from that mental attitude when that is how he was raised, but it was very confusing for me.

My earliest memories are of me at four and five years old, with my dad in his wine cellar, stacking bottles upon bottles of fabulous wine. This was what my father considered a father and son bonding experience. By six-years-old, I could tell you that I really liked *Mt. Eden* and *Kalin*, but preferred *Hanzel* and *Kistler* because of their buttery tastes. As different as my father and I are, we are in many ways very similar. He too was quite precocious when he was a young man. In fact, to this day, other than my dad, I have still never heard of a twenty-year-old boy walking around USC, smoking a pipe and bringing fine wine to college frat parties. So the bottom line is that, when I was growing up, I bonded with my dad over expensive wines, great Cognacs, Cuban cigars and his collection of exquisite pipes, beyond the wine, there were also the vacations and the food, the food!

By the time I was six, I could not only tell you the difference between good and great wines, but I could also tell you my preference between Beluga, Osetra and Sevruga caviar. Dinner with my parents on a normal evening could consist of steak tartar or crab cocktail to start, lamb chops with mint jelly, followed by strawberry short cake for dessert. Meanwhile, the other "normal" kids my age were eating pizza, Mac and Cheese, or chicken tenders and their parents were more than content to enjoy these meals with them.

Dinner at my house was always in the dining room. If my sister Dana wasn't joining us for dinner, we might eat in the breakfast room, but my parents took family dinner very seriously because it was a time for all of us to get together. Our housekeeper left by five o' clock and my mother always cooked dinner by herself. My dad would go down to the cellar to pick out a good bottle of wine depending on what we were eating for dinner that night, and then around thirty minutes later, he would emerge with a bottle of 1970 or 1980 something or other. My mom would sip on her wine as we ate, and if it was a white, it always had to be chilled as cold as possible. She was even known to put an ice cube in her wine, which drove my father absolutely nuts!

Around seven o'clock, we all sat down and the meal would consist of my dad and Dana picking on me, throwing food at each other and my mother telling them to stop. Of course it was always playful, but Dana and my dad formed an alliance and it was my mom who was always there to fight for me.

Now I don't have actual memories of someone teaching me good table manners, but I am assuming it was my mom. An interesting thing about me is that I have impeccable table manners, in fact, probably better than anyone I know. I learned at a young age which forks were used for what and which direction to ladle my spoon when eating soup. The ironic thing is that as refined as my table manners are, I can turn them off and on in a second. My friends will always make fun of me because we can be at a restaurant and I will have a heart attack if someone is using someone else's butter knife, but if it comes down to me talking in a loud voice about someone at the next table, it doesn't even faze me.

My father has a weird sense of humor, which transferred to me, but not until later in life. An example of my dad's sense of humor would be if he said something embarrassing in a restaurant when we were out to dinner, and I kicked him under the table to signal him to stop, he would look at me and say, "Josh, why are you kicking me? You are bruising my leg," and smile.

Since Dana is nine years older than I, she had much more in common with my dad and thus I think they had a better relationship. I don't know if it was because they shared a bond over sports or my sister showed a genuine interest in my dad, but I had my mind on other things like I don't know, Givenchy and Gstaad.

On Sunday mornings my family would walk down to *Dukes Coffee Shop* on Sunset Blvd. Now this place wasn't fancy by any means, in fact it was really quite a dive, but if it was good enough for every celebrity and music mogul in town, then it was good enough for us. It is the place where every rock star goes when they have a hangover and want some really good eggs and hash browns. Now it's usually a toss-up between Dukes and Nate N' Al's, it really depends on what I am in the mood for eating. If it's a little later in the morning, it's only one place... *The Polo Lounge* at *The Beverly Hills Hotel*, my home away from home.

On Sunday evenings, we would eat outside in the backyard. Sometimes, in the middle of the meal, Dana and I would get into a yelling match and of course my father would take Dana's side. One day they thought it would be really funny to tie me to a chair and spray me with a garden hose. Everything was done in fun, but it did get very annoying at times, and made me always dependent on my mom.

As odd as my relationship with my father was while growing up, the relationship between my dad and my mom was and

16

always will be magical. It has been a match made in heaven. If I told you that in twenty-five years I have never heard them fight one single time, it would not be a lie. They are madly in love with each other and my father would do anything for my mother. I was very fortunate to grow up in a house where there was so much love between two people, and I was lucky to know that both of my parents loved me unconditionally.

Private School:
The Beginning

Even though I had attended a year of their pre-school, when we applied to get into Stephen S. Wise Temple Elementary School, I almost did not make the cut! We went to my interview for kindergarten and the first thing out of my mouth to the teacher was, "My dad drives a BMW 7-series, what do you drive?" I then started playing dress-up in the corner of the classroom. Somehow my mother managed to convince the teachers that I was normal, and I was accepted.

We were never a super religious family. We did not go to temple every week, we were not kosher and we did not celebrate Shabbat on Friday nights. However my parents wanted me to get a Jewish education and that's why I attended Stephen S. Wise. I will tell you this though, we were indeed Jewish enough that on one occasion when my mother decided to put up a Christmas tree in the living room because she thought it was pretty, we suddenly awoke that evening to the sound of my father cutting it down with a hack saw.

The first signs that I might be gay occurred during my early Stephen S. Wise years. When the other boys were wrestling and playing football, I was with the girls playing dress up and trying on pearls. I can tell you I soon became very popular with the girls. I graduated pre-school and told my mother I had to get a new sports coat for the graduation assembly. Of course all the other boys were wearing Velcro sneakers, ugly sweater ensembles and those horrendous washed out elastic jeans that were ever so popular in the eighties and early nineties. I always dressed much more elaborately than the other kids. I remember making my mother take me to Pixie Town to get new dressy clothes all the time and I loved their turtlenecks. When my parents went to Europe in the summers, I always made them bring me back silk pajamas from France; I mean who was I fooling?

In kindergarten, my mother began to make me eat breakfast before I went to school. Growing up, I hated eating breakfast; I actually could not keep it down. My mother would give me the simplest thing she could think of, such as a buttered English muffin. She would bring the food upstairs into my room because it took me such a long time to get ready. After she left the room, I would always take the English muffin and hide it behind my dresser. I did this for months, and when I ran out of space behind the dresser I started hiding the muffins underneath my bed. Eventually our housekeeper found them and my mother simply gave up and stopped trying to feed me breakfast.

I don't like to kiss and tell, but I remember sitting on the kindergarten schoolyard under the jungle gym. I was in love, or at least thought I was in love. She was my first kiss, and her name was Kate. After her came Stephanie, Bryn and many more. I used to have fake weddings with these girls at recess. We would pretend to get married and in true Jewish fashion, we would include a Hora dance. I remember it like it was yesterday. I actually remember thinking to myself, "Why am I so interested in hanging out with these girls? Why don't I play handball with the other guys?"

I remember once going with my grandma Edith to Fred Hayman's, which at the time was still called Giorgio's, to buy a gift for Bryn, my girlfriend of the week. I bought her some little things

20

that I thought were essentials for a seven-year-old girl to have. You know, like a pin that read, "Fred Hayman," and an Hermes scarf. I loved going to Giorgio's with my grandma Edith. Marguerite was her sales lady and I would sit there for hours and watch my grandmother buy the most beautiful things that only Fred had. Fred used to have a bar in that store where you could drink espressos out of tiny demitasse cups, or if you were up for it, a gin and tonic with a lime. It was a different time when service was service. I am happy that I got to experience the glamorous days of Fred Hayman and Jack Taylor, when Rodeo was Rodeo. Soon after, Rodeo changed and the independents couldn't compete against the rising rents and the European fashion houses that were taking over. Even Fred Hayman, who was truly responsible for turning Rodeo into an international tourist destination, decided it was time to leave. It was very sad when he closed up shop and leased his 10,000 square foot site to Louis Vuitton in 1998.

Jamshid and the Seven Swans

My first Persian acquaintance growing up, was a boy who also went to Stephen S. Wise, by the name of, well let's call him Jamshid. For the record, many of the names in this book have been changed so I do not embarrass these people. I remember one day, Jamshid came to school and told me he spilled something in his backpack. I told him to go into the bathroom and clean it up. His idea of cleaning it up was spraying an entire bottle of Paco Rabanne in his bag. I knew then that this boy and I were going be good friends!

I remember the first time I went to Jamshid's house. He lived on the 800 block of Foothill in Beverly Hills. My mom dropped me off for a play date and I rang the doorbell. No one answered, no mom, no housekeeper, no one. I pushed it again and then after a few moments, I heard a loud buzzing noise that sounded like a dying animal on the side of the road. His door had a buzzer, no not the front gate, the front door! The French doors slowly released from the latch and opened automatically and in complete synchronization, it was like Ali Baba's palace. The only thing missing was a court jester and ten men with golden trumpets. I was now in the middle of a marble foyer that looked like something out of the movie "Clueless," but far tackier. I remember thinking to myself, "Am I supposed to announce myself?"

After waiting for a while, I started to explore Jamshid's house, which at the time seemed extraordinarily large, but when you are little everything seems big. This was the first time I had ever seen plastic on furniture. Every couch and seat was covered in a thick plastic and made of petite-point. The living room was set up like a throne room with chairs in a big circle and a massive armchair in front of a giant hearth. There were replicas of 18th century French clocks around the house and there were Persian rugs in each and every room. Atop the stairwell hung a large French Aubusson carpet. But it wasn't the gilded clocks and angels, the acanthus leaves in the metal work, or the marble driveway, which fascinated me the most, it was what was in his backyard, swans! No not swans made of gold, but seven real swans floating around in a pond. Fascinating, and my first taste of "cultural" decor. I guess, in hind-sight, it was better than the lady on the 700 block of Alta who was raising chickens in her backyard, but that's a whole different story.

The Marriage of Figaro

I remember one day in kindergarten, I wandered off the schoolyard back to the classroom by myself and no one else was there. I started snooping around and exploring, and after nothing of interest caught my attention, I reached for the door handle to leave. As I did so, some booger-picking child in the hallway accidentally slammed the door on my middle finger. I remember thinking to myself, "Isn't this the kind of tragedy you just hear about happening to other people and you feel sorry for them? This kind of stuff is not supposed to happen to me." I sat there for a few moments assessing the situation while my finger bled all over the linoleum tiles on the classroom floor. After coming to the conclusion that I did not feel like getting into trouble for wandering off to the classroom by myself, I got a First-Aid kit out and repaired my finger on my own.

My entire childhood, I was always more comfortable around adults than I was around children. I used to love to hang out in the nurse's office and the nurse and I would chat for hours on end. I used to bring her food from home and she loved my mother's meatloaf and pork chops. Speaking of pork, my mother used to send me to school with ham and mayonnaise sandwiches until one occasion when she got a call from the school administration telling her she was to cease and desist from packing any pork products for lunch. It was a kosher school and they would have none of it.

One day a teacher began to lecture me on my ham and mayonnaise sandwich and the "dangers" of eating pork. I knew this woman was not Jewish and concluded she was in her early to mid-seventies. I also determined that she was originally from Germany. The woman said to me in her thick accent, "You-are-not-allowed-to-bring-ze-pork-to-dis-school." I looked at her in the eyes and replied, "Where were you during the war?" She got the message and I walked away eating my sandwich mind you, I was not even eight-years-old. From then on, my mother had to sneak in the sandwiches for fear that I would be expelled from the school if another incident like that occurred.

The reason I used to love to hang out in the nurse's office was not because I had an affinity for medicine, it was not because I wanted to be a doctor and it certainly was not because I was interested in watching Allen, the boy with diabetes, come in to get his finger pricked every day. It was because I didn't really have many friends. The guys thought I was weird because I always hung out with girls, and as I got older, the girls thought I was kind of weird too. I mean once I "pretend" married and "divorced" all of them, they didn't want to take me back.

I also used to hang out with teachers, janitors, school administrators, anyone who would "talk" with me, and even "talking" wasn't a requirement, as long as they would pretend to listen. Parents of other kids in my class, they loved me! For the ones that couldn't tell I pitched for the other team, they were thrilled because they thought their daughters were going to marry me. For the ones who could tell, they wanted me to come over to their houses and help them redecorate their living rooms.

Teachers in elementary school also took a liking to me because I would sit there and talk to them and actually show them that I was interested. Most kids at that age want nothing to do with teachers, but I really showed them that I liked them. I remember one time learning about Jewish folk music in one of my Hebrew classes and before I knew it I was dancing on the tabletop with my teacher. All the other kids thought I was so weird, but I had a blast because I had danced these dances so many times with my grandmother. It wasn't just with the teachers, when I got much older I would dance with random parents at Bar-Mitzvah's, as if the other kids did not think I was strange enough.

I remember during a talent show one year, performing *The Marriage of Figaro*. I knew all the words perfectly because I had listened to it so many times in the car with my dad. I want to remind you that most of the things I have told you thus far occurred before the second grade. Precocious a bit, maybe? I considered doing Aida, but that would have taken too long.

My mother taught me how to read when I was in kindergarten and I have vivid memories of the two of us sitting at the dining room table reading books together and forming sentences. Being that my mother was a UC Berkeley graduate and a teacher before she became a lawyer, she made it very easy for a little boy to learn how to read. Because my mother is inherently an educator, I still find her teaching, whether it is to the housekeeper's son, or a young cousin of mine, or even to a poor child in East Los Angeles. I can't tell you how many times I came home during high school and found my mother teaching random children how to read at our dining room table.

It was clear when I was in first grade that I could not concentrate and that I was completely unfocused. I started going to tutors, and learning skills with teachers' aids. Unfortunately, this didn't work. I was then diagnosed with A.D.D. (and yes, the real A.D.D, not the kind that everyone says they have so they can get a prescription for Ritalin or Adderall from their shrink.) Ritalin started being used for young children who had attention or behavioral problems in school, and I started taking it when I

29

was six-years-old. I didn't get my A.D.D. from out of the blue, I inherited it, and it clearly wasn't from my mother!

I remember before my dad started taking medication, he had a bit of a temper. Now he takes a combination of pills, a cocktail per se, which calms him down, helps him focus and makes him a much more pleasant person overall. While he didn't show much of his temper at home, it was clearly seen elsewhere. When I listened to him at the office or on the telephone or with my grandmother in his office, the form of communication between the two of them was one tone, screaming. Talking was not even a consideration. It must be an Eastern European thing. My dad would sit there in his plush leather chair, my grandmother pacing back and forth in front of his desk, and the two of them barking back and forth. When things escalated, my mother would intervene because my grandmother's secretary was too scared to get involved. Regardless of this unpleasant form of communication, something worked because they ran an extremely successful business.

I remember one instance in particular when I saw my dad's temper in full force. My parents and I were leaving a movie and were in a parking garage when some young guy was speeding around the corner trying to impress his girlfriend and almost ran me over. Angry, and rightfully so, my dad told my mom to stay with me as he ran up to the guys car, stuck his arm in the window, and held him by the neck. He was almost arrested for battery, and it was at that point that my mother knew that my father really needed medication. He has been "sedated" ever since. So it was my diagnosis of A.D.D. that taught my mother the miracles of medication

Unlike most children, I wanted glasses as a child. In fact, I lied at the optometrist's office in order to get them. Of course the doctor could see through my ruse, so he refused to give me a

30

prescription. Years later I was shocked when I actually had to go to the eye doctor because I really did have astigmatism. Today, I would do anything not to have to wear glasses. So to say that I was "affected" is quite an understatement. If I was not singing opera at the talent show, or if I wasn't wearing turtlenecks in the middle of summer, something was definitely amiss.

For the Love of the Game

Baseball has the great advantage over cricket of being sooner ended. -- George Bernard Shaw

In an effort to launch my career as a young "athlete," my parents started me out with swimming lessons. Friends of my parents who had young kids would all get together and take turns swimming at each other's houses. One day, swim lessons would be at my house, another day at someone else's house and so on. A kid in my swim group was the nephew of a really famous female pop star. One day we went swimming at this boy's house and afterwards went to the pop star's house, who at the time was living in Mulholland Estates. This was one of the first times I remember being impressed with somebody else's home. We drove up to Mulholland Estates and the guard let us in the gated community. It was so cool because this was when this singer had just become a huge pop superstar. She was the hottest thing on the radio and sitting and chatting with her at her house was the best. She made all the kids popcorn in her kitchen and we had a blast. She took us on a tour of her house, and I remember thinking, "For a new construction, this is amazingly high quality," no that's a joke. I remember thinking, "Boy, I am one lucky kid."

I was always a huge fan of outdoor sports, just kidding! I hated all outdoor activities I even hated the beach. I didn't like the ocean because it was too cold and I didn't like the sand because it gave my feet a rash. When I used to travel to Hawaii for Christmas vacation, my family would stay on Maui. My mom, dad and sister would go down to the pool every day. Where would I be? Well if I wasn't at the Fendi or Prada stores in the mall next to our condo complex, I would be in the air conditioned room watching *Rear Window* or *A Clockwork Orange* and gorging myself on Ahi tuna and Mahi-Mahi. This was also during a time I like to refer to as "the cheeseburger summer." I think every child goes through it sometime in his or her life. For a short period of time, I thought that it was okay to eat chilidogs and cheeseburgers every day after school. By the time I realized you couldn't do that and stay thin, I was twenty pounds overweight. Needless to say, I knocked off those pounds in a matter of months and have kept them off ever since.

As I mentioned, I had these swim lessons. But it wasn't only swim lessons, it was Gymboree, soccer, basketball and tee ball, you name it and my parents tried to interest me in these activities. None of them appealed to me. When I was seven-years-old, my dad taught me how to ride a bicycle at Roxbury Park. Growing up, my parents did everything they could to raise a "normal child." Teaching me how to ride a bicycle was only one of many small attempts, and it was these activities, these horrendous activities, almost as probing as an IRS audit, that made me realize, God, I hate sports!

When I was seven, my parents enrolled me in Beverly Hills AYSO, which stands for *American Youth Soccer Organization*. When I tell people I played soccer for five years, they are usually quite impressed. I follow up the first statement by telling them that during my tenure, I only scored one goal, and it was for the opposing team. My friend and former team mate, Zach reminded me that we would sit on the soccer field in the middle of the soccer game and pick grass and watch dump trucks drive by. I really hated soccer and my father constantly reminds me that I

34

would say to him on the way to soccer, "Why are you doing this to me?" I was talking about our soccer days with Zach the other day. He said, "Look whose laughing now!" Zach too, is doing very well in real estate. He is working for his grandfather, who is a well-known real estate developer in Los Angeles

My mother was always the best when it came to supporting me in whatever I did. When I played soccer, or attempted to play soccer, the mothers would trade off bringing snacks for the kids in between the games. Most mothers brought oranges or Chewy Bars and Gatorade. My mother brought dozens of doughnuts or burgers and fries, ahh, the memories.

When I got a little older, my grandmother started giving me golf lessons at Hillcrest Country Club. We started with a lesson every Saturday morning at the club, and one of the club pros would teach me how to swing. I actually became decent enough, and I stress the word decent, that I could play in the clinic with the other kids at the club. We would all go out together and I shortly became known as the kid who would play four holes at eleven in the morning before going in for a steam at twelve. I was good enough that I could eventually shoot a 120, on the front nine of the course. It was pure luck one day, when I hit a ball, which in turn hit a tree, which in turn hit a fence, which in turn bounced off the fence and became a hole in one. I was already aware of the custom that, "he who hits a hole in one has to buy drinks for everyone." The only problem was we were all well below the legal age to drink.

With golf also came tennis lessons, but those lasted only for a short while when my parents realized that the only reason I liked the game was because I got to wear Lacoste polo shirts and white shorts. We also tried T-ball and then baseball. My experience on the diamond lasted for one painful year until my parents

35

finally realized it would be better to take me out of the game than embarrass me any further. Finally when I got a little older, my parents found my calling. A sport that I did enjoy and that I actually was good at, ballroom dancing, (as if this wasn't a big enough clue.)

Some of my fondest memories growing up were on the Cotillion dance floor, gripping the overweight bodies of perspiring girls with no rhythm or poise. I used to carry a handkerchief in my suit pocket just to wipe off their sweat. Cotillion was my passion. I was always made fun of by the other boys because of how excited I was by it. As much as they made fun of me though, I did not care. I won every single dance competition and while those boys were scoring goal after goal on the soccer field, I was waltzing away to one of Tchaikovsky's scores, and believe me, as much as they made fun of me, they wished they could dance like I could. When I got on the dance floor, everyone's eyes in the room were on me, and it is a feeling I will never forget. At one point, the teachers actually could no longer give me awards because it was upsetting the parents of the other kids. It was not a surprise to my mother that I was such a great dancer, after all my grandfather was an incredible dancer, and so is she. So in addition to things I would inherit from my mother, such as getting a nose job at fifteen, dancing would be added to the list. I remember the teacher of Cotillion fondly, because she was always winking at me and giving me that look of "You go boy, you are the only one in this room who can dance."

At the end of the year, Cotillion would culminate with a dance at The Beverly Wilshire Hotel and all the kids would dance for the championship. What was most fun, was when all the boys had mother and son dances, and my mom and I showed them a thing or two. As good of a dancer as I am, my mother is really amazing. We got up there and everyone watched us. There was

36

nothing stopping us and my mother would whisper in my ear the whole time, "You're doing great, but just get that pretentious look off your face!" Every year, I would take home the gold. When my parents saw how much I enjoyed dancing, they started giving me piano lessons, then acting lessons and then of course theatre camp, which brings me to my greatest early passion, Greystone Mansion.

Greystone Mansion: The Greatest Inspiration in my Life

God is in the Details. -- Ludwig Mies van der Rohe

In 1926, Edward "Ned" Lawrence Doheny Jr. began construction on what was to become the greatest estate in Beverly Hills and possibly on the West coast. Greystone, still remains the grand dame of Beverly Hills, almost impossible to replicate, and by far, way too expensive to ever duplicate. Greystone has 55 rooms, 12.58 acres (originally 429 acres) and 46,054 square feet, and was only enjoyed by the owner of the house for four months. In February of 1929, Ned and his secretary Hugh Plunkett, (who was rumored to have been a homosexual who had an interest in Mr. Doheny) were found shot to death in what appeared to be a murder-suicide. After the gun shots, it took three hours before the police were finally called to the mansion, and exactly what took place during that time still remains unclear to this day. After the homicides, Mrs. Doheny moved next door to a smaller mansion (only 25,000 square feet), which she called "The Knoll." When Mrs. Doheny sold the Knoll, she moved into a 6,000 square foot luxury apartment in the same building my grandmother Margie lives in, The Wilshire Terrace.

By 1963, the city was in negotiations to purchase Greystone and they cut a deal for it in 1965 at a cost of $1,300,000.00. The city leased the property to the American Film Institute (A.F.I.) for $1.00 a year, and in return the Institute would maintain Greystone. A.F.I. left in 1982. I remember the first time I visited Greystone. My mother drove me up to the property and we walked around the estate for hours. I can still remember looking through the windows in wonder at this magnificent estate. I was truly in love for the first time in my life, and this was real love. This was the first time I had ever seen anything like it. In fact, there really aren't too many houses that I have seen to this day, which hold a candle to Greystone.

Greystone had a summer theatre camp run by the City of Beverly Hills. The private camp, which was called Catskills West, ran from June to September. I attended Catskills for roughly seven years, and they were seven of the best years of my life. At Catskills, I participated in many theatre productions including *Guys and Dolls*, *Winnie-the-Pooh*, (where I played the lead role as Winnie), and *Alice in Wonderland*. I loved every bit of it, but mostly I was happy because I was at Greystone. The group of kids at Greystone was very interesting and I remember many of them well, in fact, a lot of the people I know today I met when I was a little boy at Catskills Camp. I remember one kid in particular, let's call him Michael, and even though I did not know what it was exactly about him at the time, there was something different and it was very pronounced. He used to walk around in tight clothing, had a lisp and wore a heart shaped diamond ring. The writing was clearly on the wall, but for a young kid like myself, I really didn't understand it. I don't think Michael even understood it. I believe Michael was the first gay boy I ever met. But even when I could not tell what made him different, I was different too.

I remember once at Catskills, I wandered off from our group, and before I knew it, I was giving a tour of the property to some tourists from Europe. The property is a public park, so anyone can visit. I remember all the counselors looking for me and when they finally found me, I was giving a tour of the grounds to a couple from Belgium.

Greystone became an obsession for me. The Doheny's and the Doheny family history became my passion. I lived and breathed Greystone and it was my favorite topic of conversation. I learned everything and anything there is to know about Greystone. While at camp, I was asked to give the Beverly Hills Mayor, Vicki Reynolds, and the City Manager, Mark Scott, a tour of the mansion. To me, it was the biggest honor ever. Greystone was not only a passion, it was a part of me. I would sit up in bed late at night with the lights off, trying to go to sleep, and I would think about Greystone, and I would pretend that I was Edward Lawrence Doheny Jr. and that Greystone was my house. I started to imagine what I wanted my house to look like when I was older and I would build my imaginary home in my mind. Most of the inspiration came from Greystone, and I started to draw this house.

Within a few years, I had a full architectural set of plans, down to the art and furnishings I wanted for this estate. I would imagine what I would have in this house, from the pattern of the marble floors, to the design of the finish work, to the cars that were parked in the garage. I made lists of every single car, from Packards to Cords, to Duesenbergs and Rolls Royce Silver Ghosts. When Jacqueline Kennedy passed away, my father brought home the Sotheby's catalogue of the items her estate was auctioning off. I researched that book tirelessly and copied and took notes of every piece I wanted in that book. The fact that the auction was in a month and I was talking about hopefully purchasing things thirty years in the future meant nothing to me. Another fact I did not

41

take into account was that it would be hard to find a property that could accommodate ninety cars, but none of that mattered. I did not have a care in the world and nothing was going to stop me from my dreams. I made my father take me to a bookstore and he bought me dozens of books on cars, art, interior design, architecture, and the homes and history of Los Angeles. Greystone was such an inspiration to me; it really was what made me fall in love with homes and with real estate.

It is no surprise that when I had my Bar Mitzvah, I called up the City of Beverly Hills and asked them if we could film my Bar Mitzvah video montage at Greystone. To film at Greystone, you need to apply for permits, which is a lengthy process. They allowed me to bring a film crew to the property and bypass the permit process entirely. When I got much older, I decided to give back to this special place and joined *The Friends of Greystone*, which is the Board for Greystone.

Herman and Margie Platt

*You know you're getting old when you stoop to tie your
shoelaces and wonder what else you could do while you're
down there. -- George Burns*

Their home was photographed in magazines and they had the
most gorgeous garden in the entire city. Even at a young age,
I loved going over to Grandma Margie and Grandpa Herman's
house. My father called Margie Duchess because she looked like a
duchess and she had the air of being from a royal bloodline. Going over to Margie and Herman's house, and then to their condo
at The Wilshire and then The Wilshire Terrace, has always been
fun for me because my grandmother Margie has a wonderful
sense of humor and an incredible disposition.

The Platt family is very famous in Los Angeles because of their
contributions to Jewry, no not jewelry, but Jewry. Members of the
Platt family (my mom's side,) have been residents in Los Angeles since the early 1900's. I am a third generation Los Angeleno.
My grandfather Herman was CEO and Chairman of Platt Music
Corporation, a national retail chain started in 1905 by my great-
grandfather, Benjamin Platt.

My great-grandfather Benjamin arrived in the United States
in 1905 when he was only twenty years old. He was born in a
small town near Kiev, Russia, which is now Ukraine. He started
his career in New York City as a salesman for the Singer Sew-

ing Machine Company. He moved to Los Angeles later that year and started Platt Music. He began by selling pianos door to door and by 1926 Platt Music's annual sales volume was in excess of $3,000,000, a huge amount of money back in the 1920's. My great-grandfather built three buildings on Broadway in downtown Los Angeles. 620-622 Broadway (next to the Orpheum Theatre), 830 Broadway, and 834 Broadway, which today still bares the Platt family name. Walker & Eisen was the architectural firm that designed the buildings. They are best known for designing the Beverly Wilshire Hotel in Beverly Hills.

In 1926, my great-grandfather commissioned the great African American architect Paul Williams to build his home. He gave Williams one of his first major jobs in Los Angeles. By 1928, Platt Music was a successful retailing operation but in 1929, the stock market crashed and Platt Music went into receivership. Luckily, because of my great-grandfather's good relationship with Tom May of the May Co., Platt rebuilt Platt Music to be bigger than ever. Platt Music contracted with the May Co. to sell appliances in all of their stores. By 1955, Platt Music was the largest retail business of its kind in America. My great-grandfather, while well known in the business world, was mostly known for being a humanitarian and philanthropist. He was one of the founders of The City of Hope, and was active on its Board for many years. He was the President of the Jewish Home for the Aging, and was one of the founders of the University of Judaism (now the American Jewish University.) He was also the president of Sinai Temple for twenty-one years, the longest president to date, and he was active in Masonry and the Scottish Rites. He was also a founding member of Hillcrest Country Club. When Benjamin died, in April of 1960, Los Angeles City Hall shut down and adjourned for the rest of the day in his memory.

My mom's parents, Margie and Herman Platt, were also very well known in the community. Herman and Margie endowed the Marjorie and Herman Platt Gallery at the American Jewish University and my grandfather was also the president of Sinai Temple like his father before him. Herman was the president of Vista del Mar Charities and was one of the men responsible for creating Mount Sinai Memorial Park Cemetery. In 2005, Mount Sinai named its chapel and administrative buildings after my grandfather. My grandfather was also a key supporter of, and fundraiser for, Cedars-Sinai Medical Center, the Jewish Federation of Los Angeles, the Jewish Home for the Aging, the City of Hope National Medical Center and the UCLA Foundation.

Growing up I would go over to Margie and Herman's, and grandma would prepare breakfast for us, or should I say, Angie would prepare breakfast for us. Now let me explain, but first you have to understand a little bit about Margie to get in the right frame of mind. My grandmother is the ultimate Beverly Hills princess. In fact she is more like royalty. When they coined the term, "Hollywood Glamour," I'm sure they had Margie Platt in mind. My grandmother wakes up every morning and does not understand caller ID. The phone rings at 10:30AM because God forbid you call her before then. If Angie does not pick up the phone first, she answers the phone in the most Tallulah Bankhead/Norma Desmond voice one can possibly imagine. She answers, "Good morning darling, isn't it just divine outside!" Now keep in mind, it could be a plumber who is calling. Ms. Bankhead couldn't do a better job herself. My grandmother is the most regal and wildly entertaining woman I have ever met. She is in her late eighties and still incredibly attractive. Every word out of my grandmother's mouth is *darling, fabulous, and divine*. She basically invented the word fabulous. To give you an idea of my grandmother's personality, I remember when I was a little boy

47

having dinner at Trader Vic's one evening with my parents and grandparents. We were sitting in the Ship Room, a few tables over from a very famous celebrity. My grandmother had been told that she had an uncanny resemblance to this woman. Grandma Margie got up and walked towards her, meanwhile my mom was pulling Grandma Margie's jacket sleeve saying, "Mom, stop. What are you doing?" I naturally followed my grandmother since I wanted to see her talk to a celebrity. Margie went over to her table where she was having dinner and said "Darling, how are you? I'm Margie Platt and I just wanted to come over and say hello, because you know, you are my sister, I mean, how much do we look alike darling!" And believe me, every dahhhhhlingggg was exaggerated and don't forget the missing R in the pronunciation of the word.

I could see that the celebrity looked quite perplexed, but Margie grabbed her hand in that way that older women do, you know when they shake your hand but it's with the left hand and they give you that little pat. Margie then said, "Well my pu-pu's (little Hawaiian appetizers) are getting cold, but I just wanted to come over and tell you how much I adore you. Look me up. I'm in the book." It was so strange, but it was so Margie Platt.

Breakfast at my grandparents always consisted of Vienna Sausage, ketchup and scrambled eggs, which Margie always said she cooked but we all knew it was Angie's doing. Truth of the matter is, Margie probably doesn't even know how to crack an egg. When my mother was growing up, Margie had two ways of communicating from the dining room to the kitchen (which by the way was only fifteen feet away,) First there was the antique brass bell. Now in the off event that Ethie, grandma's housekeeper when my mom was a child, did not hear the bell, there was a backup plan, a buzzer. The buzzer was conveniently placed underneath the dining room table. When my mother was growing up, her friends would come over for dinner, and her childhood friend Sharon, will still tell you today how surreal it was when Margie hit the buzzer and Ethie would come out and say "Yes Mrs. Platt?"

For the first ten years of my life, I used to tool around town with grandma on errands. She drove a powder white Mercedes SL convertible with blue interior. It wasn't just an SL, it was a classic SL, and one of the cars you see in classic car dealerships that are worth a hundred times more than what they were worth when they were originally purchased. She used to drive around in big Doris Day sunglasses and she looked like Grace Kelly. My grandmother had a collection of sunglasses unrivaled by Karl Lagerfeld himself, and they were those great big Yves Saint Laurent and Christian Dior clear frames from the 1980's. I used to love looking around Margie's closet. It was like a Judith Leiber showroom in there. You cannot imagine the amount of purses, shoes, evening gowns, furs and Fendi coats this woman had, and the smell, the smell of those overpowering mothball cans that people used to put in their closets.

I used to love to take bubble baths in my grandmother's bathroom when I was a little boy. She had wonderful smelling bath oils in large crystal decanters and the softest luffa sponges. After I would get out, I would dry off and go shopping. Shopping you ask? Shopping referred to what I would do when I would go into her storage room in her attic. Even in that little warm room under the roof, she had the most exquisite Asian pieces of art. I can still remember the smell of that room. It smelled just like what you would imagine an attic would smell like. I would pop out of the attic and say "Grandma, can I have this piece of tortoise?" or "Grandma, can I have this little pre-Columbian number?" She would always respond, "Sure honey, but don't tell your mother or Nancy I gave it to you. Do you still have that Ming jar I gave you?" I told you, this woman is fabulous!

My grandpa Herman reminded me of Irving "Swifty" Lazar. He had the most gorgeous clothing. He was a shorter gentleman and wore big tortoise shell eyeglass frames. He always smelled of Old Spice, and he had over one hundred Brioni suits. I mean this man kept Jack Taylor, Battaglia, and Giorgio's, in business. While he was pretty quiet and you thought he wasn't paying attention, he would always interject a dirty joke into a conversation. He had great rhythm and he was a wonderful pianist and a fabulous dancer, not to mention a great painter. Unfortunately I did not know the active Herman Platt because he had his first of many strokes when I was very young. He lived until he was ninety-five years old and Margie really kept him going. They were madly in love and my grandmother lugged him around with his red walker always saying, "Come on Herman, faster!" He would always yell back, "Quiet Maga, his nickname for her, I'm ninety-four years old, what do you want me to do, run?"

My grandparents, after they were robbed at gunpoint, moved from their home to The Wilshire. The thieves took off with all my grandmother's jewels and left them afraid to live alone in a big house. From the Wilshire, they moved to the luxury Wilshire Terrace. The interesting thing about The Terrace is that it is probably the most understated building on the Corridor. I'll guarantee you have never even paid attention to it when driving by, yet it has more extremely wealthy people living in it than any other single building on the Wilshire Corridor and probably in all of Los Angeles. The reason why you might ask? Well, because you can't just waltz in the front door of its magnificent lobby and say, "I would like to buy a condo here." Oh no.. it's a co-op and it's the only one of its kind in Southern California. It's a place where your family name is almost as important as the money you have in the bank.

If you don't mind sacrificing some of the amenities that newer buildings have to offer, for the prestige of the Terrace name (not to mention its own in-house hair salon and real wood burning fireplaces in every unit,) then it is the only place to go. It is a building where if you read through the public records, you will find the names of past owners such as Mrs. Doheny, Mr. Billy Wilder, Ms. Rosemary Stack, Ms. Suzanne Pleshette and Mr. Tom Poston. It is not uncommon for resident's names to begin with Sir or Ambassador. It is truly a special building.

My grandfather died in January of 2005 at the ripe old age of ninety-five. He was in remarkably good condition for a man who had suffered so many strokes. His funeral service was at Forrest Lawn at Mt. Sinai Memorial Park and he was buried in the cemetery he and his cronies were responsible for establishing. He led a truly remarkable life. I know the accomplishments of my great-grandfather and my grandfather and I know how important their contributions to the City of Los Angeles and to the Jewish community are, and I am extremely proud of it.

Eric and Edith Flagg: High Cotton

I was very fortunate to come from two great families, the Platt's and the Flagg's. Ever since I was a little boy I idolized my grandmother Edith Flagg, because she represented everything that I wanted out of life. When I was really young, I already knew that I wanted her Rolls Royce and big fancy penthouse. My grandmother inspired me from an early age to work hard, "because what you want is attainable," she said, "but only if you are willing to work for it."

I asked my grandma one time what her first memory of me as a child was. She told me that when I was three-years-old, I had pooped in my pants while sitting on a table in her kitchen. She came in and could smell something was wrong. I turned to her and before she could say anything I said, "Do you mind excusing me please? I need some privacy."

While I do not actually recall this event, it sounds like something I would have said. The first memory I have of my grandmother however, is not sitting on the table in her kitchen pooping, but sitting on the floor of a toy store kicking and screaming because I wanted a toy. We were walking to the movies and I ran into a toy store because I saw something I liked in the window. My grandmother who was trying to teach me that you can't always have everything you want, repeatedly said no. She finally took me outside of the store and sat me on a bench. She said, "Now we can be friends or we can be enemies. I am not going to buy you that toy no matter how hard you kick and scream. So we can have a nice day, or we can have a bad day. It's your choice." I realized she was not going to buy me the toy so I figured if I shut up, I could probably get popcorn out of her at the movies.

Other memories I have of my grandmother are going to The Armand Hammer Museum, to L.A.C.M.A., to The Norton Simon and to The Huntington Gardens. I really enjoyed spending time with her and learning about art and culture. Unlike most kids, I loved going to museums. I still remember going to the Catherine the Great exhibit at The Armand Hammer when I was five. I remember seeing Catherine's gilded carriages and I remember the impression it left on me. Because my grandmother exposed me to this at such a young age, the outcome is that I learned an incredible amount about art and art history.

My grandmother has a very unique story, so unique that I wrote and published her biography *A Simple Girl: Stories My Grandmother Told Me*. My grandmother is a holocaust survivor and was a member of the secret Dutch Underground Forces in the Netherlands, a group that saved Jews and non-Jews in Nazi occupied Holland. She was originally born in Romania, but moved to Vienna at the age of fifteen to pursue a career in fashion. By the time she was nineteen, Hitler had marched into Vienna, and almost overnight, Swastikas were appearing everywhere. My grandmother saw the writing on the wall, so she packed up and got out of dodge. But she didn't run back home. She wanted freedom and she was not going back to the sheltered life of Romania. Instead she followed her lover Hans, and went to Holland. My grandmother joined the Dutch resistance and got pregnant with my father. Her first husband, Hans Stein, my grandfather, was killed in Auschwitz. She knew Eric Flegenheimer, who was also a member of the Dutch resistance, and they married and raised my father together. The three of them came close to death many times, but miraculously survived the war.

When the War was over, Eric traveled to America and my grandmother went to Palestine with my father. They stayed in Palestine until it became the modern state of Israel and then they boarded a steamship for America. My grandmother had only three dollars in her pocket, she actually had five but my father got hungry along the way. My grandmother worked a few jobs, and shortly made some money, not a lot of money, but enough so they could have food on the table. My grandmother and my father met up with Eric in Los Angeles and made a home in a garage they rented in Hollywood. Trust me, it wasn't the Ritz. My grandmother slowly became known in the community as a successful freelance designer of woman's clothing. With $2,000.00 saved, my grandparents opened Edith Flagg, Inc. in 1956. Within ten years, it became an extremely successful clothing manufacturing company. My grandmother became a very respected designer but it was not until 1967 that she really hit the big time.

In 1967, my grandmother was traveling through Switzerland in search of new fabrics. She came across a material that felt like wool yet was washable. The minute my grandmother found it, she knew she had something. Long story short, the material was called Polyamine. My grandmother brought it to the United States and within months, she turned it into the most popular fabric of its day. That fabric is also referred to as *Polyester*. So in short, my grandmother became incredibly successful and was single handedly responsible for the horrendous synthetic fiber jogging suits of the 1970's.

The interesting thing about my grandmother is she does not look the part of a successful businesswoman; in fact she looks far from it. If you were to see her walking down the street, you most likely wouldn't even give her a second look. She is four feet eleven inches tall and usually wears a baseball cap and oversized sunglasses. She looks like a character out of a movie and when you talk to her, you realize what a character this woman really is.

I used to love going to my grandparents penthouse for dinner. They had a housekeeper named Lucille who would entertain me until my grandmother got home from the office. Sometimes my grandfather was home before my grandmother, depending upon whether his card game at Hillcrest had finished early. I would go over and grandpa would be sitting in his maroon leather chair. We would sit and talk and he would try to impress me with all of his accomplishments and achievements in life, many of which were fabricated, but I pretended to be interested. After about an hour of that, he would teach me how to sing German beer hall songs from the fatherland. He would then teach me profanities in German and tell me to go up to people at Hillcrest he did not like and repeat them. When people asked me to translate what I had said to them, I was to tell them the truth, and make sure to let them know who told me to say it. My grandfather was an eccentric man, and he made sure that he let everyone know what he thought about him or her. He had, what you would call a *shtick*, and it was just so Eric Flagg.

For instance, when I was younger, my grandfather drove a white Cadillac convertible, but in later years decided to play it down and drive a beige Chrysler convertible. At the same time, my grandmother had no interest in cars and basically was forced by my grandfather to drive a Rolls Royce with the license plate *Puiu I*, which in Romanian means "little chicken." One after another, he kept making her buy Rolls Royces while she would have much preferred driving the Chrysler. That man was a character and you either loved him or hated him.

My grandparents and my dad owned an office building to-gether, 400 S. Beverly Drive, on the southeast corner of Beverly Drive and Olympic Blvd. in the heart of Beverly Hills. After my grandfather retired from Edith Flagg, Inc., he did not want to retire completely, so he ran The Flagg Building. In my grandfather's typical egotistical style, he let the world know he owned one of the biggest office buildings in Beverly Hills by putting a big neon sign on the roof, which read "FLAGG." The only signs that could possibly compare in size were those on Broadway in New York City, and if he could have, I'm sure he would have made the sign sparkle as well. My mom and dad were mortified. I can remember, to my mother's relief, when they got a call that the City of Beverly Hills wanted to take down the sign because the letters were too large. Thanks to my mother, the sign was down the next day. The funny thing about that building was that for the first ten years they owned it, my grandmother was never in it once. She was just too busy running the family business downtown.

When I was ten years old, Edith and Eric decided to tell me over dinner outside on the terrace of their penthouse, that my grandfather, Eric, was not really my biological grandfather. Lucille had just cleared the table and in between our entrees and dessert, my grandfather proceeded to tell me about Hans, my real grandfather. I broke down and cried, I felt like they were telling me I was adopted. I later found out that when my father was around the same age, they told him in a similar way that Eric was not his biological father. My grandfather and father were playing gin rummy and when my grandfather gave him the news, my father simply responded, "Are we gonna talk or are we gonna play cards?" And that was the end of that conversation. Just as my dad considered Eric to be his real father, I always looked at Eric as my real grandfather.

After my grandfather retired from Edith Flagg, Inc., his routine became the following; he would go to The Flagg Building around 8 AM and stay there for four or five hours. He would then leave and make one of two crucial decisions, Malibu or Hillcrest? He would then hop into his little tan convertible and either head over to Malibu where he would have lunch at Geoffrey's, and then jump into the Pacific Ocean, or he would head across the street from his house to the Hillcrest Country Club to play cards with the boys. When I say "the boys" I am referring to George Burns, Marvin Davis and Walter Matthau.

Hillcrest Country Club has been my home away from home for twenty-five years, but to explain to you what it means to me, you have to really understand the connection I have with the place. My great-grandfather, Ben Platt, was one of the founding members of the club and in 1924, my grandfather Herman became a member at age fifteen and my grandmother Margie is the longest surviving member of the club. Herman was at one time the vice president of Hillcrest, and I would not even be here today if it was not for Hillcrest. You see, both of my grandmothers fixed my parents up in the lobby of Hillcrest.

Grandma Margie was passing through the lobby of the club when she bumped into Edith. They started chatting and Margie told Edith she was having lunch with her daughter, Cindy. Edith was about to play golf and she decided to miss her tee time to stick around and see what Margie's daughter looked like, she had a hunch that it would be worth it. Edith took one look at my mother and knew that this was the girl for my then, forty-year-old bachelor father. My father was a playboy and my grandmother incessantly put pressure on him to get married. When she realized he wasn't ready to settle down, she took measures into her own hands. My mother will tell you, "This woman who was less than five feet tall came up to me in the dining room of the club and started looking me up and down. She was inspecting my teeth, my legs, even my boobs."

Within a few moments my mom knew what was going on and later that night, she got a phone call from my dad. My father took her out on a date and on that very first date, my dad drew a map on a placemat of where he wanted to take my mother in Europe. My mom thought this guy was full of crap and was just handing her a line. Four months later they were in Europe where my dad proposed to her and three months after that they were married, at Hillcrest, of course.

This was a huge step for my father who was with a new girl every week until he was forty. In fact, I don't think there was a woman in Beverly Hills that he didn't sleep with. Many times my mother, my father and I would be walking around Beverly Hills and all of a sudden we would hear, "Michael! How are you? It's been so long!" from an anonymous woman. My mother and I would know exactly what was going on, and after the woman left, my dad always said, "I can't remember who in the hell that was." Mom and I of course knew that it was one of his former girl-friends and would just laugh our heads off.

Some of my greatest memories as a child were going with my grandparents to Santa Barbara where we would stay at the Four Seasons Biltmore Hotel. We would drive from Los Angeles on a Friday morning in my grandmother's car. I would sit in the back-seat, my grandmother in the passenger seat and my grandfather would be behind the wheel blasting German beer hall songs. It was quite interesting, to say the least. My parents would follow behind us and we would drive through the morning haze until we hit the turn off at Olive Mill Road. My grandparents were very good customers of the Biltmore and we were treated very nicely. We were very good friends with the General Manager of the hotel and my grandfather, who was the biggest flirt on the planet, would always work his magic to impress her. We would arrive at the hotel around noon and before we knew it, we were in the presidential suite of the Biltmore.

When I got a little older, I would split my summer vacations between theatre camp at Greystone, and a Jewish camp in Malibu called Hess Kramer. I used to get teased because I would always arrive at sleep away camp a week late because I would be in Europe with my family. My grandmother would then drive me up to Malibu in the Rolls and drop me off in front of the dining hall. You can imagine how much the kids teased me. I think it was at Hess Kramer that the weird side of me as a child came out. You see, this was the first time I ever really had much interaction with lots of kids. Of course, I had been to nursery school and years of middle school, but going to Hess Kramer, I now had to live and interact with other kids for three weeks. Let's just say that I came very close to being kicked out of Hess Kramer on more than one occasion. I would run around the cabin naked yelling and laughing. Then I would sneak out at night and go to the girls' cabins to try and get some action. I was always unsuccessful. I think at the time, I may have really been torn between my sexuality.

The same time that I went to Hess Kramer, my sister Dana was working as a counselor for the camp. I think that is the only reason they let me stay. She had been a camper there for years, and then became a counselor. I don't think they could believe that I, the weird troublemaker, was actually Dana's brother. Another memory I have of camp was the letters and packages I received from my mom. She would write me letters every single day. I would really look forward to those letters and packages..

I definitely did not know I was gay (for sure), until I was in middle school. As a kid, I did have feelings for girls, especially at

60

Camp Hess Kramer. I remember many girls who I liked and was genuinely attracted to. Even outside of Hess Kramer, at Stephen S. Wise, there were girls I liked, aside from the girls I would get "married" to on the schoolyard. There was one girl in particular, her name was Ashley. I had such a crush on her, and I think even though I did not know I was gay, girls like Ashley must have known. After all, I could dance, I liked to shop, and I liked to give girls gifts. My guess is that they must have known well before I did.

My grandma Edith really shaped me, in fact people say we even look alike. People think she wears a wig, but if you look closely you can see that her hair is real. She does have an extraordinary wig collection though, but for different reasons. In the 1970's, Edith Flagg, Inc. had a strike and many of the company employees picketed the building. Things got a little violent and to disguise herself, she would go downtown every day in a wig. Oh yeah as if a 4 foot eleven inch woman in a wig getting out of a silver and black two toned Rolls Royce with a customized license plate that appeared to read POOP wouldn't bring attention to herself. But it made her feel safe to wear it and no one stopped her. I suppose in a certain sense, she was reliving her war years, going under cover. That is the real reason she would do it. In fact, there is actually a funny story.

When the strike started, my grandmother called the police down to Edith Flagg, Inc. and sat them in her office. She sat back in her big armchair and said to the men, "Look, you don't know me, but don't let my appearance fool you. I may be less than five feet tall and I may only weigh ninety pounds, but I beat Hitler, and I am going to beat these people too. I still have the first dollar I ever made and I intend to win this strike." The officers were shocked. She then asked her secretary to recruit some men she knew from East Los Angeles to serve as her bodyguards.

61

She became so close with the guys that she used to put them in sports coats and ties and take them to Hillcrest for dinner. And as my grandmother said to the policemen, she did indeed stop the strike.

Aside from looking alike, my grandmother and I act very similarly. I, however, have no right to act this way, because contrary to her, I did not come to this country with two dollars in my pocket. Let me explain. My grandmother has no problem staying in the finest hotels in the world or blowing a bunch of money at Neiman's, but she will not pay for valet parking. My grandma is the kind of person who will eat caviar off of a paper plate because she would rather not run the dishwasher or make the house-keeper do extra work cleaning up after her. My grandmother is the kind of woman who would park her Rolls Royce three blocks away so she won't have to pay for valet parking. When you are a self- made person, you are more appreciative of the dollar. In this way I try to emulate my grandmother and many of my friends make fun of me. They even call me cheap. They have no idea though that I am not cheap, I just know what the value of a dollar is because I too have now earned it.

Upon closing the business in 2001, my grandmother and my father had numerous offers from other manufacturers to buy their business. They subsequently turned all offers down because they did not want anyone else using the family name. You have to remember, my grandmother built her business from the ground up and her name meant a lot in the garment industry. I remember those days well, when my grandmother was the queen of the industry. She was and is, one of the most respected California fashion industry executives. When my family closed the business, which they ran for close to fifty years, it gave them time to finally relax and retire. While my grandmother still finds it strange that she no longer goes to the office every day, it's a good thing because she has more time to travel and do whatever she wants. My father is retired as well, but has become very successful in buying and developing shopping centers and other commercial properties. He also spends a lot of his time doing charity work, traveling and playing golf.

Beyond being successful in business, my grandmother and my grandfather were great philanthropists and like my other grandparents the Platt's, they too were extremely generous in the community. Over the years, they have given millions of dollars to mostly Jewish charities. My grandparents, along with Carol Burnett, were the 1971 recipients of the "Brotherhood Award" by the National Conference of Christians and Jews. In 1981, the United Jewish Welfare Fund's Apparel Division honored them with the prestigious "Morse Award", and in 1982 they were honored by Magen David Adom (Israel's Official Red Cross Service.) My grandparents were honored in 1985 by the United Jewish Fund, and then became members of the Board of Directors for the Jewish Federation Council in 1988. In 1991, they were named on the City of Hope National Medical Center's Gallery of Achievement. My grandfather was on the Board of Directors of the City of Hope from 1970-1990 and was also a vice president of the City of Hope. My grandfather along with my grandmother and parents have permanent plaques at the Jewish Federation Building on Wilshire Blvd. In 1997, my grandfather was diagnosed with cancer. He was supposed to only live for two months, but made it two years. On August 11, 1999, he passed away.

63

High Times

*I am a passionate traveler, and from the time I was a child,
travel formed me as much as my formal education.*
-- David Rockefeller

I remember when I was growing up, that for a good three or
four months out of the year, I was at home with just my mom
and Dana. My dad would travel for weeks on end to our factories
in China as well as other places in the Orient. My dad also had
showrooms in New York, San Francisco, Dallas, Chicago, Char-
lotte and Miami, which was fortunate for me because I got to go
on a lot of fun trips. My first memory of getting on an airplane
was when I was four or five years old. Things were different back
then and everything was a lot less intense. I remember sitting in
the cockpit of a Boeing 737, on the pilot's lap, and pulling back
on the gears as we took off into the sky. Don't forget, this was
pre 9/11 and terrorism in the sky wasn't something we thought
about. There weren't even locks on the cockpit doors. Smoking
was not fully banned, however the process was in the works, and
by the time I started flying, very few planes still allowed smoking, especially on domestic flights. I do recall however those little
ashtrays, souvenirs from a time when flying was still glamorous.
Those were high times.

The very first trip I took was to New York. My dad had an office
on 7th Avenue, which he opened when he was in his twenties. My
dad needed to visit the New York office four or five times a year

and my mom and I would go with him. While my dad went to the office, my mom and I would walk around the city and visit all of her favorite spots. My mother was a schoolteacher in New York and lived there before she became an attorney, so she knew where to take a young boy on his first trip to the city. You know, Rockefeller Center, The Metropolitan Museum of Art, The Museum of Modern Art, The Frick and Henri Bendel. It was a blast!

We used to stay at the Peninsula, and one evening I had my very first taste of oysters. I sat at the oyster bar with my dad and he taught me the difference between West Coast and East Coast oysters and the way they must be eaten. To start with, you can garnish them with lemon if you like, but the most important thing when eating an oyster, is the way it sits in your mouth when you put it in. He demonstrated by ordering a half a dozen, and we sat there as he taught me the distinct art of eating an oyster. First you put the oyster in your mouth, then you take three bites, let the animal slide around in your mouth and then swallow. I took that first bite and I loved it. So I proceeded to order a dozen more. All of a sudden, I threw up all over the bar at the Peninsula, but believe me I will never forget how much I loved my first taste of that oyster.

It was 1994 and my parents were going to Europe. Ever since I can remember, my parents vacationed in Europe for three or four weeks during the summer. I was ten years old and my parents were going to take me along. We were having dinner one evening on Sunset Blvd. at Le Dome (now BLT,) and I started acting up and jumping up and down on the tables. My parents and the waiters could not control me and it was right then and there that my parents realized there was no way they were going to be stuck with me for four weeks in Europe. My tantrum ruined my first potential trip to Europe; instead I stayed with Grandma Edith while my parents went off on their own.

In 1998, I was just turning thirteen and it would be my Bar Mitzvah very soon. My dad and mom said I could either have a big party or a trip to Europe. Knowing that I would be able to manipulate them later, I said I would rather have a trip to Europe. I knew that by the time I got back, I would be able to convince them that no matter how nice my trip to Europe was, it wouldn't be the same if I didn't have a proper Bar Mitzvah party. Well what was supposed to be a small eighty-person party turned into a two hundred-person bash at the Four Seasons Hotel. Do you think I didn't know for one moment what I was doing? By now, manipulation was my forte. I was already planning my party on the Cote d'Azur.

On my first trip to Europe, we went to Ireland, France and Italy. It was on our trip to the South of France that I really fell in love with the country. We stayed in Cannes at the Carlton Hotel. I had never seen anything like it before in my life. Just to give you an idea of how glamorous this place is, my mother wore a dress to her fiftieth birthday party in Los Angeles, and I saw a woman wearing that same evening dress to the beach at the Carlton! There is a pecking order at the Carlton beach and based on your years at the hotel, you are placed in certain chaise lounges along-side the beach. We would always sit near a wonderful couple from England who happened to be a Lord and Lady. My parent's good friends, Donnie and David, would also vacation there and they really became my first gay friends. I felt very comfortable around them. I think at this point, my mom thought I might be gay, and it made her happy to see how comfortable I was around these two men, who, even still to this day, are like my uncles. Either that or my mother was completely oblivious. I mean for fun, I used to like to go over to my gay uncles house and do Tai Bo.

For my father's sixtieth birthday, my parents invited forty friends to the South of France and my dad had the most wonderful party on the beach of the Carlton. The party started at sundown and lasted well into the night, with the most wonderful food, the greatest musicians and magnificent wine. Everyone had the best time. Everyone got really dressed up and we all celebrated his birthday at tables on the sand. It couldn't have been a better party. Those were definitely high times.

The Misfit

Youth is a wonderful thing. What a crime to waste it on children. -- George Bernard Shaw

I have very few good memories of middle school. In fact, I really don't think I have any, so I will try and sum up this period of my life in as few words as I possibly can. I graduated from Stephen S. Wise and started Brentwood School in the fall of 1998. I was now thirteen-years-old and I had been one of the oldest kids in my class. I had the choice of continuing on at Stephen S. Wise High School, Milken or attending Brentwood School. I chose Brentwood. Looking back, this probably was not the best choice I have ever made, but on the scale of poor choices I have made during my life, this is low on the totem pole. However I do remember this being a difficult choice. During the summer of 1998, I waited every day for the mailman to deliver the mail to see which schools had accepted me. I impatiently waited until finally I got my responses back from the schools. Since I did not attend university, I can only imagine these are the same feelings of anxiety that high school students experience as they wait to hear which colleges have accepted them.

I remember seeing the envelope from Brentwood School with a star sticker on the back. I opened it and was thrilled to read that I had gotten in. Now I had to decide if I should stay where I was familiar, or venture on to new territory. My parents did not influence me and let me make this decision on my own. I made a pro's and con's list, I made diagrams, graphs, and I weighed out my choices with percentiles. Finally, I made my choice to leave Jewish school, and go to Brentwood School. Wrong choice, but I guess you never know how your life would have turned out had you chosen differently. Frankly, I was very unhappy at Brentwood School, I felt like the kids and teachers wanted me there just as much as I wanted a bullet in my knee.

My first day at Brentwood School was quite a different experience. I had attended Jewish day-school all of my life. There was an hour of Hebrew class and an hour of Bible studies every day and Shabbat services on Friday afternoons. The biggest choice I had to make was if I would have regular challah or challah with raisins! To go from that environment to a secular school was monumental. At Brentwood, there were white kids, black kids, Jewish kids, Christian kids, Asian kids, rich kids and poor kids. In many ways this change of environment was very good for me. I know many kids that continued on in Jewish school that were never exposed to anyone other than Jewish students.

I felt utterly overwhelmed those first days at Brentwood. I truly did not know a soul. Four years earlier, my sister had graduated from Brentwood School before going on to Duke, so I did know some teachers, but with the exception of the director of the school and faculty members that had known my sister, I did not know a single person. Even though I did not know anyone, and even though no one knew me, I could sense from the beginning that this would be a major uphill climb in order to be liked.

From day one, I felt tension and I could sense that I was not liked. At orientation, very few kids wanted to hang out with me and it was pretty clear that day who the popular kids were and who were going to be the losers. Clearly I was not going to be one of the popular kids. This was strange for me because even though

72

the boys made fun of me at Stephen S. Wise, I still felt like I belonged. In an effort to get to know my classmates and gain social standing amongst my middle-school peers, I invited all of them, (along with my friends from Stephen S. Wise), to my Bar Mitzvah that December.

In a series of parties commonly referred to as "Bar Mitzvah Central," seventh and eighth-graders spend the next few years of their lives going to different Bar and Bat-Mitzvahs every Saturday night. We'd party on Diet Cokes and Shirley Temples, (and in some cases, gin and tonics.) I don't know how I pulled it off, but getting alcohol from the bar tenders was never an issue for me. In fact, despite how young I looked, even when I was hedging on twenty-one, I rarely got carded because of the way I talked.

I was so intent on making new friends that I invited everyone I could think of, and frankly was not even sure who they were. By the time of the party, I realized I did not even know everyone's names, and I invited a bunch of the wrong people. The other day I was watching the videotape of my Bar Mitzvah . It was so interesting upon reflection, to see how all the kids that were at my party turned out. The popular kids really did turn out to be the losers; the ugly ducklings really did turn into beautiful swans, and that Lebanese boy who used to call me a fag now wears dresses. Too bad I didn't know all of this would happen back when I was so preoccupied with making new friends.

Now there is no doubt that as a child of thirteen or fourteen, I was no less obnoxious than I was in my former years, however, I believe fourteen was the first time I ever heard someone refer to me as an instrument used to clean a woman's vaginal region. A "douche" was a term I would hear frequently for years to come. I was unequivocally a total and utter snob and the word braggadocious when describing me was an understatement. The only time

I was ever noticed was when I was being made fun of. I guess I deserved a lot of it. I think the underlying issue was that people realized I was gay, and being gay then (even though this was only ten years ago,) was not the same as being gay today. Kids have it a lot easier today, than I did. Today it is no big deal to come out in high school. Back then, it was unheard of. So I guess you could call me somewhat ahead of the times.

I digress. I do remember thinking to myself, "These idiots don't think I am cool, but I know I am cool!" Despite the way they treated me, I never had a low sense of self-esteem and never had the sense that I was a loser, like many unpopular kids do. One thing I always had throughout my life, even though I was very insecure, was self-confidence. I just couldn't figure out why these kids hated me. Looking back, everything is very clear, but during the moment, you don't see things the same way. I did not let the way these kids treated me convince me that I was a loser or anything less than. I knew I had everything going for me, so I refused to let myself fall into the "loser" category. You are only a loser if you let yourself feel like one and I never felt that I was a loser. I was not going to fall into the category of the guy who goes to the school dance with the ugly girl and sits in the corner and no one talks to them. Instead, I just did not go at all. I pretended I was too busy, yea too busy clipping my fingernails. And it was this attitude that made me visible during class, but when the bell rang, I was gone. I would do my own thing, by myself, and I would walk with my head high. The one thing I never let anyone do, was feel sorry for me. I never let anyone think I was bothered or that my feelings were hurt because I did not want to be a pity case. But beleive me, I was bothered, and it is true, high school really does suck. Even so, at all times I walked fast as if I had somewhere to go, and I pretended that I didn't have a care in the world about

74

anyone else. Of course though, I couldn't wait for the day to be over.

While I always knew I was different from the other boys, it took me until I was thirteen or fourteen-years-old to really figure out what made me different. I knew I liked Broadway shows, the Golden Girls, French antiques, my mother's jewelry, and had an unhealthy fascination with my grandmother Edith. Even my mother just thought it was a part of my personality. I mean after all, my father loved shopping with my mother for women's shoes and he loved clothing, so some of my shticks were really not that outlandish. It should have been a clue to my mother though when at eleven, I knew the difference between Japanning and Chinoiserie.

When I was thirteen and puberty started, I was confused for quite some time. I tried to convince myself that I liked girls and truly made myself believe that this was the case. I ignored the facts that I would rather hang out with my gay uncles, Don and David, than watch a sporting match. I convinced myself that I was a normal girl- loving guy and that I would be able to get over this "phase." As do all boys, it is at this time in a young man's life that they discover their hands are not only used to write with and hold things with, but can also be used to, yes, just use your imagination. So I remember, "discovering" this great diversion for the first time when I was either twelve or thirteen years old.

At first I would think only about girls, but then those darn boys would just keep slipping into the back of my mind. I tried to ignore them, but things were just not working out my way. So I then came up with a solution to this problem, or shall I say, a compromise. Mondays, Wednesdays and Fridays would be days I would think about girls while taking my forty-minute showers. Tuesdays, Thursdays and Saturdays I would think about boys. I

75

can't remember what happened on Sundays, but I assure you it wasn't anything freaky. Well after a while of this game, I started thinking, "Eh, it's not such a big deal if I skip a day and think about boys instead of girls. No one is going to know I thought about boys instead of girls this one day aside from me." And after a bit of this it started to be less frequent that I thought about girls, and eventually I erased girls from my mind all together. Of course they would come in and out on occasion, but 90% of the time, I was only interested in guys. And then came the feelings of guilt. Even though I came from the most open-minded family you can ever wish for, there were still feelings of guilt. I don't know if guilt is the right word, but I knew boys liking boys was not normal and all I ever wanted to be my whole life, was normal. I thought to myself, well I can always get married and no one will ever have to know I like guys. I can just keep it a secret. But then I thought to myself I did not want to live with that kind of a lie and I did not want to lie to someone who loved me.

But if you thought I was fully convinced I only liked guys, I wasn't! If I was going to go the other way, I was going to make one hundred and ten percent sure I didn't like girls, so what did I do to find out? Aside from ordering every *Girls Gone Wild* DVD, I slept with a slew of girls but I will get to that later.

My Very Own Grandma Mame

If you're contemplating getting married, take a trip with your partner. If you come back and neither one of you has killed the other, it's a match made in heaven.
-- Joshua Flagg

So what does a boy do, with no friends, on a Saturday night? He hangs out with his grandmother. As I mentioned before, my grandmother Edith was my idol as I was growing up. I loved my grandmother's lifestyle and I wanted to emulate her. I still do to this day. I think she is the coolest woman on the planet, mainly because she says what is on her mind and she does not care what you think about her. I like to think of myself the same way, but in reality, there is no one I know like my grandmother.

I remember one time a few years ago, while riding in the car with her, she was wearing her usual sneakers and hat and said, "Do you want to go to the Beverly Hills Hotel for dinner?" I said, "Sure why not, but let's go home first and get dressed." She said, "We are dressed, don't worry, they will take my money." She had no qualms about walking into the Polo Lounge in sneakers and a hat for dinner; in fact, she loves doing that kind of stuff. The woman just does not give a damn about what anyone thinks of her. It is interesting,, my entire life people have been telling me that the relationship I share with my grandmother is so special. I know it is special and unique, but to me, it is just normal. Being friends with someone who is sixty five years older than I am does not feel weird to me. It feels great.

Now as you can probably tell, I have been close to Edith since I was a little boy. When Eric was alive, he and Edith had a fantastic social life so she could not spend as much time with me. However, after a two-year battle with cancer, my grandfather passed away. It seemed only natural that we both started spending more time with each other, and let me tell you, the best way to stay young is by hanging out with old people! I don't know why everybody doesn't do it?

For the next three years, my weekends consisted of going to dinner with Edith at Hillcrest, The Beverly Hills Hotel and the Bel Air Hotel. Sometimes I would even stay over at her penthouse afterwards. We had a blast together. So during this time, when my other middle-school companions were starting their high school career, you know, house parties, drinking, smoking, first sexual experiences, I was listening to Antonio play Vivaldi on the piano in the bar at the Bel Air Hotel with my grandmother. Would I trade this for anything? Never!

My grandmother was eighty-years-old and I was fourteen, but the fun did not end there. My grandmother decided to take me traveling, and boy did we travel! She decided to take me everywhere in the world she had already been, and in eighty years, as you can imagine, that's a lot of places. Even if she did not care to ever return to a particular destination, she did the most selfless thing and took me there because she wanted me to form my own opinions. We traveled to every continent, just me and my grandmother. Sometimes we would bring friends or family, but for the most part, it was just the two of us doing the same thing in different places around the world.

The two of us have traveled to more than sixty countries together, and we still take two or three big trips every year. The only thing that has seemed to change over the years is that I have gotten taller and she has gotten shorter. These trips have been more productive and informative than any college education. Seeing the world and experiencing it first hand is more important than anything you can ever learn in a textbook. Reading about the politics of a country is one thing, but seeing it and living it is another. I am not saying education is not important, on the contrary, it is most important, but if you can combine a good education with years of travel, this is the best way to form a well-rounded and intelligent person, at least that is my opinion.

On one trip, Edith and I traveled to Buenos-Aires and stayed in the world famous Alvear Palace. At the time it was not safe to go outside at night, so it was there that I decided one evening, in our hotel suite, to start writing my grandmother's life story. During that trip I can remember one evening in particular. The sun was setting and we were sitting at an outdoor cafe. It was Hanukkah and a group of rabbis were outside lighting a giant Menorah. They recited the prayers on a loudspeaker and it began to drizzle. They then proceeded to sing and dance the Hora, and one thing about my grandmother, is that when she hears that music, she needs to dance. So there we were in the middle of the street, now pouring with rain, and my grandmother and I with about two hundred other people, were all holding hands and dancing the Hora. Everyone was in such a festive mood. It was such a wonderful moment, and I will never forget singing and dancing in the rain, holding hands with the people, Jews and non-Jews, of Buenos Aires.

On another trip we traveled to Munich. Afterwards, we drove to Austria and I will never forget the unbelievable scenery. The drive to Vienna is one of the most gorgeous drives in the world. On the way we visited Graz and Salzburg and finally arrived in Vienna. We stayed at The Imperial, one of the grandest hotels in the world, and I took pictures of my grandmother standing on the famous staircase that Hitler had once walked down. It was kind of her way of saying he was dead, and she survived. She then showed me the avenue where Hitler marched into Vienna. We walked down the avenue to where she and her sister Martha were standing, and Edith described the Aanschluss.From there we traveled to Budapest where my eighty-year-old grandmother and I walked over a bridge across the Danube River and crossed from Buda to Pest. The Danube is not just a little river, by the time we got to Pest, I could not walk any further. She of course, was ready to climb up a hill to show me a view of the city.

One of my favorite trips was with Edith and her sister Martha, when we went to Romania. We traveled there to see what remained from her childhood, which unfortunately was not much. Everything was so dilapidated and antiquated. We took a group of thirteen people to dinner in a very nice restaurant and the bill was twenty U.S. dollars. I hear the economy is different now, but back then, it was unbelievable. We then took a car and driver and traveled throughout Romania to visit the places she lived and vacationed as a child. Sadly, everything was gone. Romania is pretty much a third world country, so this was not one of our most glamorous trips, but it was remarkable seeing the expression on Edith and Martha's faces after they had not been home in over sixty-five years.

Another year, my mom, my dad, my grandmother and I decided to go to Israel. Of course this was not my grandmother's first time, after all she lived there when it was still Palestine. My father however, had not been back since he was a six-year-old. Due to my family's involvement with the Jewish Federation, they made VIP arrangements for my family on our trip. When we arrived we had an armored limousine pick us up at the airport. We spent a few nights in Tel-Aviv and from there, a car and driver took us all over the state of Israel. We saw it from top to bottom in two weeks. We stayed at the King David Hotel in Jerusalem, which was spectacular. The suite overlooked the Wailing Wall, which was lit up beautifully at night. The evening we arrived at the King David Hotel, I was a bit hungry, so I went downstairs and sat on the terrace of the hotel with my grandmother. We ordered soft-boiled eggs as we sat outside and stared at the wall. It is a wonderful memory I will never forget.

On almost every trip I take with my grandmother, in the middle of it, we change our itinerary. We both cannot be in the same place for too long, so after a few days we leave and go somewhere else. It is not uncommon for us to be in one country, and instead of staying in the vicinity of the area, taking a plane and traveling to a different continent completely. One time my grandmother took me and my friend Matt to Egypt. We went there and the first day we arrived, my friend Matt asked her, "What should we do today?" She replied, "Well first we will have a cup of coffee and then maybe we will see the pyramids." Everything with her revolves around coffee. We had lunch at the Mena House and then went to see the pyramids. After a day of the pyramids, she got bored, so we hopped on a plane and flew to Venice and then to Milan, even though it was the dead of winter. The following year, we returned to Turkey for a second time. I took Matt with me again and after two days of bad weather, we got on a plane and left for Florence. That's my grandmother.

Recently, I told my grandmother I had to do something for work on the east coast. She said "Well you'll be half way to

83

Europe, why don't we have coffee in Paris?" Before I knew it, we were in Jordan, Morocco, Cap d'Antibes and Paris.

Growing Up: The Good, The Bad and The Raunchy

I can remember when the air was clean and sex was dirty.
-- George Burns

To say that my recollection of most of my high school career is a bit hazy would be an understatement, however there is a great deal which will be seared in my mind forever. I know it sounds like they were really terrible times, but in actuality they were the best of times. When people tell you to appreciate your youth, they know what they are talking about. Looking back now, the words that come to mind when I think about high school are reckless, invincible, entitled, indestructible, grandiose and committable. Now I am not going to sugarcoat anything here, and as I have mentioned before, what good is writing a book if you can't be honest. So judge me if you like, but please don't tell me you were perfect in high school.

People did not like me for several reasons. For one, they did not understand me. There was something different about me that they could not put their finger on. When the kids were playing football outside, I was gossiping with the girls. When kids talked about their trips to Disney World or the Grand Wailea, I was talking about the great evening I had with my parents at Maison du Caviar in Paris and how much I enjoyed the George V in

Paris. I have a lot to thank my parents and my grandparents for because they gave me an incredible life, but I definitely did not have a childhood in the normal sense. I did not grow up like a normal kid and considering I did not go to college, I really never had a youth. I was born and all of a sudden I was a forty-year-old man. Am I happy about it? Yes and no. I am happy because again, I have been so lucky to do things that people only dream about, but at the same time, my entire life, and even today, I feel like an outsider, I never felt like I fit in. The biggest problem was that I was so different. I didn't know at first that I was gay; I just thought why am I considered so unusual. It is hard to explain to someone who is not gay, so I will try and do the best I can and see if you can follow me.

The stereotypes for homosexuals for the most part are true. Why? I don't know, but many gay men do have certain likes and dislikes that straight men don't. As a child, fun for me was sitting at Giorgio's and watching my grandmother go shopping. Or, fun for me was going to see an opera or a Noel Coward play in New York, or the Phantom of the Opera when it was at the Music Center in Los Angeles. Fun for me was playing the part of Nathan Detroit in "Guys and Dolls" at theatre camp. So there I was, a young gay boy with very few friends, and I didn't know anyone my age that could relate to me. I was like a forty-year-old stuck in a twelve-year-olds body.

So I would go to school, get made fun of, have a horrible time, and then come home. Luckily, I eventually found a new group of friends I would go out on the weekends with other fun kids from Beverly Hills that had similar interests that I had. Within a short time, I established a network of friends. You can't try and fit in with a group of people if you have nothing in common with them. It will never work and I am sorry that it took me so many years to figure this out. Instead of trying to fit in with people who

88

I had nothing in common with, I should have looked for people I had things in common with much earlier.

My new group of friends, like me, loved to go to the Polo Lounge, and that became our spot. Every weekend for breakfast, lunch and dinner, I was there by myself or with my friends. I know this sounds crazy, but if you ask anyone who works at the Polo Lounge, they will tell you that before I started bringing my friends there, The Polo Lounge at The Beverly Hills Hotel was for old people. After a while of bringing my friends it became a trendy hotspot for young people. And it is for this reason that whenever I walk into the Polo Lounge, they treat me so graciously. I have been going there since I was a little boy and when I walk in, they make me want to come back again and again. It was funny, one time I came in for dinner with my parents and Wallid the maitre d' said, "Welcome Mr. Flagg." My dad went to shake his hand and he walked past my father and shook my hand instead.

When I was fifteen-years-old, I decided to get my first nose job. Notice I said first. I was blessed with a typical Jewish nose and I was tired of it by the time I was fifteen. Now two days after my nose job, I was getting what we call in Yiddish, Shpilkes, which essentially means, I was getting really fidgety and I had to get out of the house. So with my nose in a cast, I decided to leave my house, and walk over to the Whiskey, where I presented the bouncer with a fake ID and proceeded to go clubbing. It gets better. A few days later, I decided I had enough with the cotton packing in my nose, and thought I could play doctor on myself and take my own stitches out. Big mistake.

After I took my packing and stitches out, my nose came out crooked, so I went in for nose job number two. This time I did not take the stitches out, however I still was not satisfied, so I

89

went in for a third. Upon my third nose job, I thought to myself, "Well since I'm having my nose fixed once more, I may as well have my ears pinned back," and that is just what I did.

My friend Kathy was at the outpatient center with me and she will tell you how much I enjoyed the morphine drip. Believe me, doing your nose and ears at the same time is not exactly a walk in the park. Every time the nurse tried to take the morphine away, I became very unpleasant. For someone who has had as many procedures as I have, it's a miracle I didn't come out looking like a freak.

Cars, Cars and More Cars

When I was fifteen, my dad took me up to Greystone and let me drive around the parking lot. I then took my driving lessons and on my sixteenth birthday, I got my license. Now that I was licensed, I could drive places, I could see people and I could stay out late.

I was one of the first kids in my grade to start driving, and for the first six months very few other kids had their licenses. After all, I was always one of the oldest in my class. All of the kids I knew got the typical Brentwood kid car, either an Audi A4, a BMW 3 series or if they were really cool, an Escalade. It was at this time that my father decided he was going to treat me exactly the same way his father treated him when he was sixteen. In an effort to instill values in me, (as he and my mom had been attempting to do their entire lives,) instead of getting me what all the other kids had, he gave me a 1992 Lexus. Mind you this was 2001! He said there was nothing wrong with it and that when he was a child he only had a bicycle. He then proceeded to tell me that the happiest day of his life was when he got a nickel for shinning Elvis Presley's shoes at the Hollywood Roosevelt Hotel. I was in no mood for stories, I was ticked off that he was going to make me drive a ten-year-old car while he was driving a supercharged Jaguar convertible, my mother was driving a Mercedes convertible and our "spare" was a Range Rover!

My dad did not have money until the late 1950's, so until then he was eating baked beans out of a can and hawking newspapers on Hollywood Blvd. Contrary to my dad, my mom was eating at Chasen's. There was no winning this battle. My mother, even though she grew up with money, had a blue ten-year-old dodge for her first car because in those days, kids did not drive fancy cars when they were sixteen. In those days adults didn't really even drive cars nicer than Chryslers and Lincolns. So my mom had the same mindset as my dad. I do not know why all of the other kids' parents did not have this mindset. Maybe they wanted to give their kids what they could not have as children. My parents thought that giving a sixteen year old a new car was ridiculous and pretentious. As much as I would like to look back now and thank them for teaching me values, in this one instance I am still irked!

Now about a year later, I was driving one of my parent's cars down Sunset Blvd, because my 1992 piece of crap car was in the shop. At the corner of Sunset and Rexford, I flipped the car, which happened to be a Range Rover. The car also flipped two other cars coming from the opposite direction. This was not a fender bender. If you have never been in a serious car accident, I can tell you it is one of the scariest things ever and all you can think about is the saying "brace for impact." The car ended up against a pole on the south east corner of Rexford and Sunset and of course the accident was completely my fault.

My mother and father came to get me and I immediately manipulated a bad situation into something that would work in my favor. They needed the Range Rover as their extra car because both my parents had two door convertibles. So I convinced them that had I been driving the little Lexus that day, I surely would have been crushed to death. Truth of the matter is that the Lexus was just as safe as the Range Rover but I made a good case for why I needed a big sturdy car to protect me in the event something like this ever happened again. And so my parents replaced that Range Rover with another Range Rover, and that was now the car I was driving to school. Sounds like a great ending to a story, right? Not so much.

I'll give you another installment in my adolescent parade of stupid mistakes. One morning I asked my father if I could drive his convertible to school. Surprisingly he agreed and gave me the keys. I was reading the book Billy Budd at the time for school and I was in a rush to get to class because I had to present my project. I was a little late to school because I took an extra-long shower that morning. Have you ever heard about dead man's curve on Sunset Blvd.? Well I gave it a new name. I drove my dad's Jag on this corner of Sunset Blvd at sixty miles per hour and flipped the car. The car ended up half way in a tree. I thought to myself, "I'm going to be late to school!" No just kidding, actually I thought to myself, "Oh crap! I just totaled another car!"

I called my parents, and my mom and dad showed up. My dad directed traffic around the smashed up car, which was now leaking fuel. My mother took me in her car and said, "You're a moron, but you're not going to be late for your Billy Budd project. We'll talk about this when you get home." Needless to say, I was never allowed to drive my parents cars again and until recently my car insurance has been anywhere from twelve thousand to fifteen thousand dollars a year.

After that, my dad was pissed off and said, "Well Josh, you're not going to drive a Range Rover to school while I wait for my car to be fixed." So he took the Range Rover back and decided to get me the worst and most embarrassing car he could possibly find. If you thought the Lexus was bad, it was like driving a Rolls Royce compared to what I had next. He rented me a white Toyota Corolla with cloth interior and literally asked the car dealer to get me the ugliest car they had on the lot. I asked the rental place if I could have one with leather and they told me my father specifi-

95

cally asked them to give me the opposite of whatever I asked for. So now I had gone from driving a Range Rover to school, to driving a Toyota Corolla. It was also during this time that the DMV took my license away. So for the next six months, I did not have a car at all! I can tell you, I would have rather had the Corolla.

After the six months of not having a license, I got the Range Rover back and of course I got in another fender bender. Now I have another point on my license and guess what, no driving for another six months! By now I had already developed a reputation of being a terrible driver, and somewhere along the way, a rumor started that I had run over a homeless person. I'm still not sure where that story came from, but I do hear it every so often, "Didn't you run some homeless man over in Beverly Hills when you were in high school?" to which I reply, "No it was in Malibu."

A year later, with no tickets or accidents, my dad orders me a BMW. How I convinced him to get rid of the Corolla, to this day I still have no idea, but my guess is I started complaining so much, that he could not take it anymore. Now of course, it could not just be any BMW, it had to have every single available option and the color combination I wanted.

Of course there were not any blue 330ci BMW's with camel interior and the options I wanted, currently in the United States. So I had him order it from Germany. I was so spoiled! It took a few months for my car to be delivered and just as my car is about to arrive in Long Beach, low and behold, once again I crash another car! There goes the BMW and there goes another six months of not driving! When I got my license back another six months later, my grandmother gave me her second car, which was a Mercedes CLK 430. Not too shabby. I tried to get her Rolls, but it seemed like I was pushing my luck, and I got nervous I would get stuck with another rental car, so I just kept my mouth closed.

Cedar-Sinai Medical Center, *United Hostesses Charity Ball*, 2007
left to right, Cindy Flagg, Edith Flagg, Josh Flagg

American Youth Soccer Organization, 1995

Dear Mr president I am an eight year old boy. My name is Joshua, I am in second grade. I had an idea. Since you'r president you can change laws. I thought that there can't be guns, Bombs, or Dinomight, Because lots of grown ups or Children have been Kiled because of guns, Lots of grownup's and children are crying because of what vilents guns do. Evry day more than 2 00000 children have been Killed in the U.S.A. or lots of places. Can you make a law that Know guns can be allowed here. I think you're a very great great great!!! man. I think you'r the best president. It would be helpful if you made this law. Try to make this woarld better.!!!

Thank you

Sincerely
Joshua Flagg

letter sent to President Bill Clinton, 1993

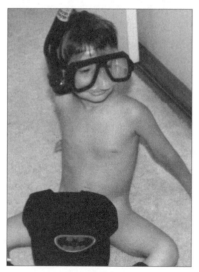

Josh Flagg, 1990

Josh and father, Michael, 1987

Flagg family portrait, 1989
left to right, Michael Flagg, Dana Flagg, Josh Flagg, Cindy Flagg

Josh and Colton, 2010

Flagg family portrait, 2010
left to right, Michael Flagg, Cindy Flagg, Josh Flagg, Edith Flagg

Josh and sister, Dana
Danas' wedding, Beverly Hills Hotel, 2008

Josh and Cindy Flagg at Josh's 21st birthday party
Hillcrest Country Club, 2006

Herman and Margie Platt
Cindy and Michaels Flagg's engagement party, 1982

Eric and Edith Flagg meet with Israeli Prime Minister, Yitzchak Shamir (left)

Eric and Edith Flagg with Carol Burnett (second from left), receive the
Brotherhood Award from the United Conference of Christians and Jews

CAMPAIGN

UNITED JEWISH FUND

UPDATE

THE JEWISH
FEDERATION
COUNCIL OF
GREATER
LOS ANGELES

Instrumental in bringing educational program on hospice movement to Southern Region are handed (from left) Audrey Harris, Jewish Hospice Commission director; Yona Kesler, regional Jewish Family Service director; Sandra Kismel, JFS social worker and bilanding; from left) Rabbi Ron Shulman, Congregation Ner Tamid; Rabbi David Lieb, Temple Beth El; and Reba Saxon, hospice commission co-chair.

Hospice Movement Focus of South Bay Series

By LISA KALMEN

Her husband was only 39 when he died, leaving her with a lot of questions to grapple with and young children to support. There was no hospice movement in those days to comfort the terminally ill and help families cope with the inevitability of death.

Thirty years later and remarried, she is finally learning ways to deal with death and dying at a first-ever series in the South Bay sponsored by several United Jewish Fund beneficiaries — the Jewish Hospice Commission, the Southern Region offices of Jewish Family Service and Jewish Federation Council — and the Hospice of California, a non-profit organization based in Torrance.

Professionals hope that the men and women attending the series will thus go on for training as volunteers to assist Jewish patients and their families and serve as liaison to physicians, nurses, rabbis and social workers in the Southern Region area, which encompasses the 40,000 Jews of the South Bay.

"Having Jewish volunteers will better meet the needs of the community," said Jane Salmon, director of volunteers of the Torrance-based hospice program, which currently has 25 volunteers countywide working in hospitals and private homes.

Noted Jewish Hospice Commission director Audrey Harris, Ph.D., whose program began in 1992 as a pilot project of JFC's Council on Jewish Life: "There's something very comforting for Jewish people to address the concept of death and dying in a Jewish atmosphere."

At the Southern Region series, rabbis Ron Shulman of Congregation Ner Tamid in Palos Verdes and David Lieb of Temple Beth El in San Pedro explained how Judaism, which values life, sanctity and preservation of life, can be reconciled with the hospice movement, which does not advocate the use of heroic measures to prolong life in the face of incurable disease.

For example, Shulman pointed out, the Talmud has recognized terminal illness with the word "goses" — which refers to impending death within 72 hours. And Lieb explained that two integral concepts of hospice care — respect for the elderly and letting the terminally ill die with family nearby

— are found in Judaism too.

"Jacob died in Egypt with his family present," said Lieb. "Until modern times, Jews always died with their family next to them."

Lieb, who teaches a confirmation class, added a mandatory trip to a mortuary when he found out that his teenage students were ignorant about death. "I found 14- and 15-year-old kids who didn't know what it meant to die. Their grandparents had died somewhere else."

Shulman is pleased that the Southern Region occasionally is taking the first forward-reaching a Jewish hospice program in the area. "I've seen the real help that hospice can give," he remarked. "In the hospital, you're just one of the people on the rounds that must be cared for ... a number in a gown in a bed. When we start a Jewish hospice program here, we won't have to say to people, 'You'll have to go somewhere else.'"

Shulman said hospice volunteers can help the dying "close their lives" by quietly making sure that a lighthouse will has been drawn and funeral arrangements made. Volunteers may want to suggest that the dying write or dictate what is termed an ethical will, in which the person discusses his life, the things he has valued, the decisions he made along the way as a legacy for families to treasure.

In the last weeks and months, Shulman explained that the dying may find solace in each "concrete things of comfort" as reciting a tefila, using tefillin and lighting Shabbat candles. The Jewish Hospice Commission believes that Jewish practices, as long as they do not contradict medical advice, can provide significant emotional support. For example, a local rabbi can arrange for a shofar to be blown at bedside and the Megillah can be read in person by a student or even over the telephone.

The commission will focus on such concerns in "Let me Help You: A Hospice Guide for Jewish Patients," a new guide to be published by the end of summer. Its editorial subcommittee consists of Rabbi Elliot Dorff, Ph.D., who also chairs the commission; physicians Lawrence J. Hollis and Geoffrey J. Newstadt; attorney David Shulman, whose concern for a dying relative made him push for a Jewish hospice

continued on page 77

Edith and Eric Flagg to be Honored at UJF Tribute Dinner

A dinner in honor of Edith and Eric Flagg and their many humanitarian achievements on behalf of United Jewish Fund is to be held at 7:00 p.m., Saturday, July 27, announced UJF Campaign General Chair Stan Hirsh.

"Here is a unique couple whose commitment to Jewish causes and Israel has been an inspiration to all of us. The Flaggs and their dedication to providing people in need with humanitarian assistance will be the focus of this extremely important UJF tribute event," said Hirsh in announcing the gathering.

Edith and Eric were both members of the Dutch underground during the period 1942 to 1945. At that time they helped bring people to safety, hiding those who had escaped from the Nazis and foraging those in need for food, health and other kinds of assistance necessary for survival.

"This kind of no-holds-barred involvement in the world would not run through United Jewish Fund today," said Edith Flagg in describing how he became involved with UJF.

"The programs and social service agencies UJF supports raise up a safety net that insures the quality of life for our community and for Israel. Edith and I feel that we have a special obligation to help make the kind of assistance possible. This is why we have been involved with UJF, Jewish Federation Council and other humanitarian organizations," he said.

Edith's sense of involvement is "behind the scenes," where she frequently helps with UJF fundraising by telephone and in person. "You have to have the stamina in order to provide the assistance," she said about her UJF work. "I help to gather the pledges which fund the Federation social service budget."

In expressing his personal philosophy about the importance of charitable giving, Eric Flagg commented, "All Jews share the same responsibility that there are Jews who recognize it and those who don't. For me it was kind of easy since I was once gassed in the Nazi concentration camps, not rescued as a member of the underground, and had nothing but good fortune after coming to this country. If after all of this, I could not live up to my responsibility, I couldn't possibly like the man I meet every day when I shave."

The Flagg's community involvement spans a lifetime, beginning more than three decades ago when they first joined the local UJF fundraising effort. Since then, Eric has

served on the Apparel Division Cabinet, as the Division's Chair, as member of the Major Gifts Committee, and, for the past four years as a member of the UJF Inner Cabinet, helping to start and plan annual UJF fundraising programs. In addition, he currently serves as Chair of the JFC Finance Committee and as a member of the JFC Executive Committee.

Eric's other community involvements include Vice President of City of Hope and member of the American Jewish Committee. Edith serves on the Merchants Club of City of Hope. The Flaggs have been honored with the National Conference of Christians and Jews. Eric Flagg was recently honored by the Israeli Red Cross.

"The Flaggs are the kind of couple to help us celebrate the meaning of humanitarian commitment and community leadership," said Stan Simons, who is co-chairing the Flagg tribute dinner.

Maurice "Bud" Schomholz, also co-chairing the gathering, added, "The work of these two inspiring people symbolizes the kind of energy and dedication which make possible meaningful improvements in the quality of life for people in need, both here in the Los Angeles Jewish community and in Israel. It is a pleasure and a privilege to be involved in planning an event on their behalf."

Sheldon Kadish is the Chair of the 1985 UJF Apparel Division, which is organizing the tribute. Lee Graff is serving as Event Coordinator.

For reservations, at $200 per person, contact JFC Staff Executive Simone Lazarowitz at (213) 852-1234, ext. 3031.

Members of community look over program materials during break in series on hospice movement.

June 28, 1985 • Bulletin • 25

Eric and Edith Flagg, honored at the UJF dinner, 1987

Edith Flagg introduces Polyester to America, 1967

Drugs and Alcohol... And More Alcohol

By now I have told you a few of my crazy driving stories, let me now tell you about some of my other reckless behaviors. I believe that I felt I was invincible. Nothing could ever really hurt me. By the time I was sixteen, I would drink wine out of a box if it would get me buzzed. The interesting thing though, was that I was always able to wake up the next day and have a normal functioning day. There were no hangovers or throwing up, although I can recall a few occasions when I woke up in an alley in Beverly Hills behind a Mexican restaurant, but that's a whole different story in itself. For the most part, I was not out of control, I just liked to party with my friends and have fun. I remember a few times going to school with an Evian bottle, which was really filled with Vodka, just because I thought it was funny. I was getting hammered in English Lit. and no one had any idea. But it was this reckless behavior that also got me into trouble and was the reason why I left Brentwood School by the eleventh grade.

Today I actually don't drink that much anymore. It gives me heartburn and I don't have the desire to get wasted like I did in high school. Maybe I am just a happier person. When I would get drunk, lots of things happened and my friends can recount tons of stories.

The first time I tried drugs I was in the ninth grade. As you can imagine I didn't start off with the hardcore stuff. The first thing I tried was Marijuana. A girl friend that was one of my few friends at Brentwood School was going to have the house to herself for the weekend because her parents were going out of town. She lived in the Palisades, and ten of us decided to get together to get stoned at her house. A couple of the kids had been stoned before so the other eight of us were trying something new. I was definitely game.

So we were all in the backyard and all of the sudden out comes a bong. I had no idea what a bong was, truthfully I thought it was a dildo when I first saw it, and thought I might have signed up for a sex party by accident. A couple of the guys loaded it with weed, filled it with water and lit it. I could not figure out what the hell I was supposed to do. So now it was my turn to hit the bong, and boy did I hit it. My recommendation for someone who wants to get stoned for the first time is to start small and maybe light up a joint. Don't rip a three-foot bong. For the record, I don't smoke marijuana anymore. Even though supposedly more than half of Americans smoke it, I don't like it.

Throughout high school, I really didn't do much besides recreationally smoke marijuana with friends. Actually that was a lie, but I would rather omit that part of my life. Let's just say I have had my share of fun. The good thing is that I don't have an addictive personality. I could try something and never try it again. The only thing I ever got hooked on was cigarettes and that was a huge mistake. One day, when I was twenty-three, I woke up and said I have had six years of this and I know if I do not stop now, I am going to end up at sixty smoking through a hole in my throat. And just like that, I quit and never touched a cigarette again. I took my last cigarette, dug a hole in the ground at The Beverly Hills hotel, and buried it.

Today I actually don't drink that much anymore, it gives me heart burn and I don't have the desire to get wasted like I did in high school. Maybe I am just a happier person. When I used to get drunk, lots of things happened and my friends can recount tons of stories. I can't give you full in-depth accounts, but I do recall certain events such as the time I went to a girlfriend's twenty-first birthday party. Now that was a party! Her parents were Russian and they had a massive Russian estate off of Coldwater Canyon in Beverly Hills. When I say massive Russian estate, let me explain the difference between a massive Russian estate and a massive estate.

An "estate" in Beverly Hills is used to describe a home of 10,000 square feet or more on at least a one acre lot which constitutes all of close to 43,000 square feet of land. A massive Russian estate is a house which fits these parameters, yet is situated on a 5,000 or maybe 10,000 square foot lot. Basically the back yard is in the living room. I further digress. The party was great, sushi station, caviar you name it, and booze, lots and lots of booze. I thought to myself, "Well these people are lovely hosts, they are Russian and I wouldn't want to offend them by not drinking, so I helped myself to a handle of *Stolie* (which by the way I don't drink any more. After traveling to Moscow, I learned that the Russians use *Stolie* to wash their dishes.) So the night comes to an end and so do I!

My friend Matt had to carry me out of the house and down the Tara-like staircase. I had driven that evening so Matt strapped me in and we proceeded back to my parents' home. We took Schuyler Road through Trousdale because he was a little tipsy himself, and we didn't want to take Sunset. We turned onto North Doheny Drive and right as we crossed North of Sunset, I yelled, "Pull Over!" Before he could even stop the car, my seat belt was off, the car door was open and I was throwing up on the pavement. Four seconds later, my head hit the pavement and I was taking a nap in my own vomit. Matt being the good friend

109

that he is, took me by the puke stained shirt and pulled me back into the car.

We got back to my parents' house and he even put me in my pajamas. Now that's a good friend, when your straight pal is willing to change you out of your clothes and put you to bed. My parents were out of town at the time so he did not want to let me fall asleep in my vomit and die. The weird thing though, was he did not put me into bed, he put me on the couch in the family room. One might ask, why? Oh well that is an easy one, because while I was drunk and passed out, he called some girl over and had sex with her in my bed and told her it was his house. At least he had the decency to nail her in my room and not in my parents. It was a great evening, or so I have heard.

Sex & Coming Out

So now that we've covered alcohol abuse, drugs, my eccentric personality and my horrible driving skills, I guess it's time to talk about sex. I mentioned earlier that I discovered masturbation in middle school, and how on certain days I would think about boys and other days I would think about girls.

When I was sixteen-years-old, I decided, I'm going to start having sex. It only took me five girls to finally confirm what I already knew, but I did indeed have sex with five girls. The first girl I had sex with, let's just say she really got around. Her name was Ann, she was Jewish, had blond hair and was very, very experienced. I knew I wasn't going to have to court her or waste my time buying her dinner to get in the sack because this girl would have sex with a homeless guy if he didn't smell too badly. Ironically, she was really attractive.

I drove from my house towards Santa Monica and stopped at a liquor store to buy a box of condoms. I kept the receipt because I knew I would want to always remember that night. I went over to Ann's house and we had sex, she was fifteen and I was sixteen. Where were her parents? Oh, they were downstairs.

After I had sex with Ann, I decided to try it with another girl, as I was still not convinced I was gay. Of course, during sex I closed my eyes and pretended the girl was a guy, but I needed more. This second girl wore me out. I remember driving back on the freeway that night and falling asleep at the wheel and just as I was about to hit the center divider I woke up. Good thing too, or I would have lost my license for another six months!

I would sneak out of my house to see these girls around two or three in the morning, and mind you this was on a school night. I would disengage the alarm system and thankfully our driveway was on a hill, so I would put the car in neutral and let it roll down the driveway to the street, all of which was scary because it was a forty five foot long driveway. When I hit the street, I would turn the engine on and go.

There was this one girl Rachelle, who lived at a house on the east side of Tower Road. It looked like a lovely home from the outside, and I wish I could tell you what it looked like on the inside. I don't know because the only room I ever saw was her bedroom. I would park my car on the street, climb over a wall and walk down the side of the house until I got to the garage. I would then climb on top of the garage roof, which was below her bedroom window, and then I would sneak inside. She would be waiting for me and we would have sex. We did this about three or four times, and every night I would sneak back out of her window, go home, and she would wake up the next morning and have Cocoa Puffs with her parents. Boy, can parents be naïve!

And then there was Alexandra. Her father was a major studio head and she lived the life of Riley. When I met her, I fell in love with her. We were soul mates. We met when we were sixteen. She was beautiful and there was an instant attraction. We had a lot in common, but what I liked most was that she was absolutely in-sane. I told her I was gay but that meant nothing to her, that's how crazy she was. I mean how many girls do you know that want to sleep with a gay man? We had a lot in common; we loved fashion and we both were complete snobs. We were a perfect match, and I was absolutely crazy for her. One day, we slept together. I don't know why, we just did it in her car. I don't know how we did it; all I remember is that my legs were up in the air.

I came out of the closet when I was seventeen years old. It was time, and I knew I had to do it. I chose to do it in what seemed to me to be the most normal place, Jack N' the Box! I was there with a girl who was twenty-seven-years-old and still lived off her parents, a guy who used to mooch off of the twenty-seven-year old girl, and a kid who was a few years younger than I was.

I was one of the first kids to come out in my private high school and I am proud to say that I had the courage to do it before it became commonplace. Today you think coming out while in high school is nothing, but let me tell you, there is such a difference between my generation, even though I graduated in 2004, and that of the generation seven years later. Today, it's fashionable to be out and proud in high school. For me, I was opening the door for the next generation. I simply said, "Screw It. I don't care what you think about me, I am proud of who I am and if you don't like me that's fine!" I was tired of pretending to be someone I was not, and I was ready to be true to myself. Do I have any regrets? Not a single one. In fact I cannot imagine living life and having a secret like that.

Around the same time, I also felt it necessary to inform my parents. One day, when I was getting myself a bowl of cereal in the kitchen, I opened the refrigerator door and as I reached for the milk, I turned to my mom, and casually said, "I just want to let you know that I am no longer a virgin." I turned around and walked out of the kitchen. My mother looked at me as I walked up the stairs and said, "That's nice honey, but whatever you do, just be safe." A few weeks later, I decided to double surprise my mother, and as I was walking up the stairs to my bedroom, my mother was walking behind me. I turned around and said "Mom, I just thought I would let you know that I am bisexual." She said, "Okay, honey, what exactly do you mean by that?" I didn't want to give her too much of a shock that day and tell her I was full on

115

gay. I told her I knew I was not straight and that I liked boys as well as girls. My mother said, "Honey, I am happy for you whatever you chose to do in your life and I love you no matter what. Just please be safe."

It was that simple. I wish I could give you some sob story about my mother crying for ten days and going to her Rabbi for comfort, but it really wasn't that way at all. I think Jews are very understanding when it comes to this kind of stuff. My mother then told my father and he came to see me in my room. He said, "Son, your mother tells me you like men." I said, "Yes, dad..." He said, "That's fine" and walked out of the room. Later that evening I went over to Grandma Edith's to tell her. I sat down with her in the study and said, "Grandma, I am bisexual." This was really someone I did not want to come out to and just say, "Grandma, I'm a homo." She said, "OK, tell me exactly what that means for you in your life?" It's not that she was asking me to elaborate. I genuinely think she was unfamiliar with the term. I explained it to her and she said, "What's new? You aren't the first one in the family to be that way. Let me tell you about your cousin Shmuli who had a thing for goats..."

My mother then told her mother, Margie. I think she was the least surprised, I mean after all, this was a woman who knew I was absolutely fascinated with her Imari collection. Within the first month or so, everyone in my family knew, and so did all my friends, and before long, just about everyone in Los Angeles. This was an exciting time for me. I knew people were talking about me, but I did not care one bit, in fact I loved it. What was really fun was seeing the expression on people's faces that had no idea whatsoever. I don't want to say that I am a real macho guy, but for the most part, I don't wear a sign on my forehead that reads GAY.

116

Now, there is a very big perk to coming out when you are in high school, one that I figured out quite early. You get to be the first for many boys who are still in the closet. I can't tell you how many boys from Crossroads, Brentwood and Beverly High that I met in secret, late at night, and got to experiment with. The best are the looks on their faces when I saw them the next day at school...you know that look of, "If you tell anyone, I will kill you." It's so interesting that all these kids that were on the sports teams, especially the kids that "loved girls," were really nothing more than a bunch of gay guys in the closet. About twenty-five percent of them came out afterwards and the other seventy-five percent still have girlfriends today. I never told anybody who they were; it's not my place to "out" anyone.

Beverly Hills High School

Now to attend Beverly Hills High School, your family has to maintain their primary residence in the city of Beverly Hills. Buying a condo for your kid or renting an apartment for them does not cut it. It also did not mean anything that my family owned an office building on Beverly Drive. It was black and white, you live in the city limits, or you don't go to Beverly High. Well my family wasn't about to let that small detail stop me

My best friend's parents owned a few apartment buildings in Beverly Hills, so my mother, who was now in a rush to get me into Beverly High, called up my friend's mother, and took whatever apartment was available in one of their buildings. My parents leased a three-bedroom, two-story apartment. We bought furniture, beds, tables, you name it, and then filled all the closets up with clothes. My mother was so paranoid about the situation that she and my father actually slept over at least two nights a week. They were not happy to do this but looking back now, the situation was really quite entertaining. On the nights my parents didn't stay over, my mom would get up at six in the morning, drive from our house north of Sunset, wake me up and then drive me to Beverly High. Remember, at this time my driver's license had been taken away. Can you imagine what amazing parents I have? My mother would cook dinner in that small kitchen, my dad would sit on the tiny terrace and smoke his cigar, and they made this arrangement work until I graduated high school. Are you wondering what happened in the apartment on the nights that my parents were at their house? Well that's a whole different story. Let's just say my final year of high school was one of the best years of my life.

On the nights where I was not under the guidance of my parents, I had reign over the apartment. I could have anyone I wanted over, I could do whatever I wanted, I could stay out as late as I wanted without having to worry about my parents knowing where I was. Of course my mom was constantly checking up on me, but the truth is, I got away with murder.

As I mentioned, the goal was for me to graduate high school. My mom knew I had no motivation, so she hired a tutor. Now this tutor was not your typical tutor. For twenty dollars an hour, he would come over to my place and do my homework. He was an eccentric guy named Brett. He did not even have a car, he rode a bicycle. To all of my friends, he just went by the name "Brett the Tutor." Brett would sleep with my girlfriends, he would sleep on the couch, he would do my homework, he was basically my personal valet (of course my parents didn't have any knowledge about my arrangement with Brett.) Rain or shine, he would be there to clean up my mess whenever I needed him, I mean hell for twenty dollars an hour, I probably would have done the same thing. By the end of the year, he had saved up enough of my parent's money to buy a car. I have to say, it was quite amusing getting stoned with my tutor, going out with my friend Stacey and having my homework finished by the time I returned. I was such a spoiled brat. Talk about naïve, my parents actually thought I was doing all of my own homework and they were ecstatic because my grades were ever improving.

By now, I was no longer sleeping with girls; after five of them I had had enough. This apartment was the location for many affairs with straight and gay boys. I had met a boy, let's call him Juan, who was from a very religious Peruvian upper class family. He

120

looked completely straight. The bond that he and I shared was truthfully over the fact that we could drink most people under the table. One Sunday night we got wasted and slept together. This was during one of the periods of time that I did not have a driver's license and my mother took me to school in the mornings. That Monday morning, my mother came to pick me up from the apartment, and found us in bed together. Let's just say it was a very uncomfortable ride to school.

I always had an entrepreneurial streak and at age seventeen, I exercised it. I decided when I was in eleventh grade to create a clothing accessory line. At the time, wristbands, sweatbands and trucker hats were really popular. I cut up my sister's Louis Vuitton Keepall and took the leather to a leather man who started making bracelets, patches and other shapes out of the leather. I would then have it stitched onto these wristbands and hats and sell them to stores. While my business never really was a huge success, the items I made were quite popular and even made it onto an episode of "The Simple Life," I guess Paris must have bought one of my hats from a store on Melrose. In any event, while I was not as successful as my grandmother in the clothing business, my grandmother supported my endeavors and I made up for it later in the real estate business.

At the end of my high school career, my mother, my grandmother and my father were elated that I had graduated high school. Now what was I going to do? Well I knew I was going to pursue a career in real estate, after all I was fully licensed by this time. But I thought I would give college at least an attempt. I figured, I would go to Santa Monica College for a few semesters and after I completed all the credits required, I would transfer over to USC. Well I gave that college thing a try for about three weeks, and after three weeks my mother noticed that all of my books were still wrapped in their cellophane covers, and all my

121

notebooks had drawings of houses in them. It was at this point my mother actually said to me, "Forget about college, it is a waste of time for you, you are never going to get through four years of this." And it was at that point I dropped out. She was right, there was no way I could have done the college thing for four years.

Even though I knew college wasn't for me, I do regret not going to college because I missed that aspect of my youth. I never got the college experience. But then again, I guess there were a lot of aspects to my youth that I missed out on because I was so different. However I am not going to lie, it really does bother me when I tell people that I did not go to college. I always have to follow that statement up with, "I went straight into business."

It is sometimes a little hard to follow the difference between my high school life and my business life, and the time line is a little difficult to understand because a great deal of it overlaps. For example, when I was eighteen, I already had the listing on a $6,000,000 house belonging to a friend of my grandmother; meanwhile I was trying to stay awake in math class after a night of drinking.

Now after reading about my exciting past, you are probably thinking to yourself, "Why in the hell would he write about this stuff?" Well the answer is quite simple. Because I am no less guilty of having a good time than any of the rest of you. If I left it out, you would think I was hiding something. I was a reckless teen and thought I was unstoppable, but at the end of the day, I finally got my stuff together. I was able to accomplish something that very few people at my age are able to do. After I graduated high school, I began to mature and within a very short period of time, became the complete opposite of what I was in high school. I was now a young businessman. I got all of the partying out of my system and I was ready to be a responsible human being. It took me quite a while, but I am a different person today. I am now a man.

123

Colton

If you live to be a hundred, I want to live to be a hundred
minus one day so I never have to live without you.
-- A.A. Milne

I have only loved two boys and one of them didn't even like me.
Well, I should say that the first boy was an infatuation. I could not
have him, and it made me want him more. The second boy is my
boyfriend, life partner, husband, whatever you want to call it. If
you asked me what my favorite thing about Colton is, it is that he
loves me and he loves me unconditionally.

The problem with this first boy was that he loved that I loved
him and that was all. He did not really care about me, or if he did,
not to the extent that I did about him. I cried for a month straight
after he told me he was not interested in me in that way. I think
I cried more because he was the first person I loved and I had
never experienced love before. I didn't leave my house for three
weeks. By the time I finally got out of the house, I looked like
death warmed over and I felt like it too. I was so depressed and
my self-esteem was lower than it had ever been before.

I remember one morning my mother took me for brunch to the
Beverly Hills Hotel. We sat outside and I really opened up to her
and told her how I felt. This was difficult for a person like me who
does not express his emotions easily.

She said, "As badly as you feel, I am happy this happened to you because I truly wasn't sure if you were capable of loving somebody unconditionally."

And she was right. After so many hook ups, I really did not know if I was capable of loving someone. I was having fun, but I just never really felt attached. Three months later, in that exact spot at the Beverly Hills Hotel, I found myself having brunch with my mother and Colton.

The minute I saw Colton, I lusted after him as I did the first moment I saw many boys. However, the difference was that Colton was very smart. He did not just jump into the sack with me. In fact he made it very difficult. I remember sitting in New York flirting with him by phone and being interested in him. It did not stop me from hooking up with other boys during that trip, but that, at the time, was just my nature.

I finally met Colton on a blind date. A girl who I was friendly with showed me his Facebook page and after I saw it, I wanted to become closer friends with this girl so I could meet Colton. Colton came over to my house on Readcrest one night with his friend Zack. When Colton arrived, he assumed, that the car parked in front was my dad's and that I lived with my parents because most twenty-two-year-olds don't drive Mercedes S 500s. It was not until later that he discovered I lived alone and everything in that house was mine.

Now the great thing about Readcrest was that if you could not think of how to start a conversation with someone, all you had to say was "is it too warm in here, if it is I'll just open the roof for you?" You see the house was built completely out of glass and was actually the large greenhouse that belonged to William Randolph Hearst in the 1920s. After Hearst passed away, the greenhouse was moved up to the location on Readcrest. The Readcrest house was interesting because it was really a small English Tudor style cottage, with two greenhouses on either side.

On the right side of the house was the greenhouse, which consisted of my kitchen, dining room and breakfast area. On the left side was the greenhouse that actually was my living room. Because there were only glass walls, I became somewhat creative and started hanging art on the panes. It was so creative I even captured the attention of a few magazines and had the house photographed for publication. Now as beautiful as Readcrest was, because of all the glass, it was stifling in the summer and freezing in the winter. As much as I loved the place, it was impossible to live there and I moved, or shall I say, we moved.

After that first meeting, and on our first night that Colton and I went out, it was with his friend Zack and this girl. We went out for cocktails...oh who am I kidding, we went out for drinks in West Hollywood. I of course was already toasted and as Colton tells it, I was the most obnoxious son of a bitch he had ever met. After almost a month of dating, we finally consummated our relationship, and a week later he moved in with me. I used to come home from work and I would be so excited when I would see his car parked in front of Readcrest. We would watch TV, then go out to dinner and meet up with friends. Slowly we started going out as a couple, and then we were almost never apart.

In 2008, Colton and I moved into a condo I bought on Avenue of the Stars in Century City. My grandmother lives in the penthouse of the building across the way and you can believe me, she was influential in getting me to move into that place. I bought a condo on the seventeenth floor and that's where we live today. I have always loved the building. Colton hates it.

127

The building has got incredible history. The building was built by I.M. Pei, a world famous architect, so what's not to like? Colton makes fun of it because we are the youngest people here and every other day another ambulance comes through the security gate. I tell him that all luxury buildings are like that but he doesn't care. He wants a house for our very ferocious dog, a little Springer Spaniel by the name of Godzilla. I am not a house person though. I love living in a service building. I mean after all I can barely change a light bulb without getting electrocuted. People are either house people or building people. My plan is one day to get a place in New York, and keep my grandmother's penthouse in Los Angeles. I don't want the responsibility of a house. I would rather have someone take care of everything for me.

I always tell Colton, "I want to die one minute before you." Colton is my boyfriend, best friend, husband, life partner, whatever you want to call it. If you asked me my favorite thing about Colton it would definitley be the way that he loves me. He is the only person that knows me inside and out, and has accepted all of my positive and negative qualities. From the moment I met Colton I knew I had to spend the rest of my life with him. The only way I can really describe it is that he completes me. The relationship Colton and I have is so great because we are so similar and yet so different. We both have the same interests, we both love to travel and see new things. But at times I do realize our differences are not invisible, and realizing that has helped me grow as a person and understand that certain things in life are a trade off. We both bring different qualities to the relationship. I love the excitement and energy he brings to my life, and I would be lost without him. Colton and I have a very unique relationship, I have never met anyone who can just make me laugh regardless of what we are doing.

Mansions and Millionaires

Every day I get up and look through the Forbes list of the
richest people in America. If I'm not there, I go to work.
-- Robert Orben

Every year, I probably get nine hundred calls and e-mails, asking me questions about real estate. I also get about four hundred and fifty hang ups, which leads me to believe that I should really take my phone number off of the public listing services. But for those people that I actually speak to on the telephone, they all want to know one thing. They all want to know how I can further their careers as real estate agents. Sounds simple, right? Their careers? I didn't know I was in the business of furthering other people's careers. Last time I checked, I was still working on my own, but nevertheless, I still talk to people, usually young realtors, my age or maybe a little older.

They always start the conversation with the same questions: "How did you get into real estate, Josh? Can you give me some advice?" Or my favorite one is, "If I move to Los Angeles, can I live with you while you teach me how to sell million dollar homes?"

Nothing surprises me anymore. I'm asked these questions on a daily basis and as I listen to these people, I think to myself, "How is it possible that all these people are looking to me for advice?" Only six years ago, I was sitting in math class in high school, barely graduating! So I often try to figure out how I did it, and truthfully, I can't say I have a simple answer. It's funny, you make one twenty million dollar sale while you're still in high school and all of a sudden you're the golden boy of real estate. I'm not a huge producer and, in fact, there are many bigger producers than I am. I'm not selling ten homes a month and I don't have a sales team. I don't employ five assistants, I don't have my own escrow department, I don't even really go into my office all that often. I work out of the house, and when I am not doing showings, I'm walking around my home in sweats and hotel slippers talking on the telephone. So why in the hell am I writing this book? Well, I have mentioned all the things I don't have and the things I don't do, but now I'll tell you what I actually have done.

I've done about $100,000,000 in sales in my best years, obviously not in 2009 or 2010. I sell homes anywhere from $3,000,000 to $25,000,000, and the homes I sell average out at a value of roughly $6,500,000. So, if I don't use an office, don't employee five secretaries, don't have an escrow department and wear my slippers to work, how do I do it? Well that's easy, I only sell ten to twelve homes a year. However, all of the properties, or most of the properties, are at the top end of the market. So how did I get such a unique and enviable job? Well, I guess the best way to tell you is to start at the very beginning, way back, six and a half years ago, to 2005.

I'm not going to lie to you and tell you I didn't have certain advantages As dramatic as I would like to make my story sound, I didn't have a father who beat me, thus inducing me to hop on a bus in the middle of the night, heading towards Hollywood where I would pursue an acting career and wait tables, before saving enough money to enroll in real estate school and pass my exam, thus getting my real estate license and sitting on other brokers' open houses until I eventually sold my very first $200,000

132

home in Riverside. No, no... it was nothing like that. Nothing that colorful. However, I can say this; I did everything on my own. I did not get my license and start selling properties to my parents' friends right away. Believe me, they weren't about to give their multi-million dollar homes to some kid who didn't even graduate college.

In 1996, my family sold their office building on Beverly Drive in Beverly Hills and in 2000, started buying up shopping centers out of state. Well, there went my plan of working for the family clothing business. Believe me; managing their shopping centers in Texas was just not in the cards. So I needed to think of something, and I needed to think quickly. Hmm, what to do? I could have become an architect. I have loved architecture since I was a little boy, but then I thought about it, and realized that it required too many numbers. I could become an interior designer...nah...I didn't want a bunch of elderly women in Beverly Hills bossing me around. So then it dawned on me, "Ahh, real estate. I am going to become a real estate agent!"

In 2004, I took my real estate classes and despite failing the first exam, I passed on round two and was now officially licensed in the Golden State, California. By the way, I only flunked by one question and the question was: "What instrument measures radon gas?" Oh yeah, like I was ever going to need to know that one, but I digress.

I remembered while growing up always looking at the real estate section of the paper on Sunday mornings, and also picking up real estate magazines every time I was out. There was always one broker whose listings stood out from everyone else's. He was not one of the big powerhouses like Coldwell Banker, Prudential, Sotheby's or Keller Williams; he was actually a one-man show. He didn't even have an office, but instead worked out of his home in

133

Bel Air. His name was Steve Myers, and he owned Steve Myers & Associates. To be perfectly honest, this isn't his real name, but as I mentioned before, I've changed many of the names of people in my real estate saga.

I would say from 1950 until 2000, "Steve" was the king of real estate. Not only was he the king, he was "it." Steve was interviewed by everyone from Walter Cronkite to Barbara Walters, and from Joan Rivers to Robin Leach. He was the supreme authority on luxury real estate. When an actor, a lawyer, a doctor, a *Fortune 500* mogul, a prince, a sheik, or even the Shah of Iran came to town and wanted to buy a property, there was only one person to call, and that was Steve. When deciding who I wanted to call and see if I could get a job, first I considered many of the bigger real estate companies. But I kept going back to those full-page ads of $20,000,000 and $30,000,000 homes in Beverly Hills and Bel Air. So, I called Steve and what do you know, I landed the job.

I thought to myself, "This is great. Not only am I going to be working under one of the greatest brokers of all time, but I am going to make so many contacts from Steve." Well, all I can say is things didn't work out exactly as I had planned. As with everything in life, it's all about timing. Unfortunately, by the time I joined the firm, the phone stopped ringing as much as it had in the past, the big listings stopped coming in, and all in all, business was very slow. I will admit, however, that the first year I started with Steve Meyers & Associates, the company still had some pretty big listings. They had the biggest house in Beverly Hills, and a famous property known as the Sheik's Property on Sunset Blvd. During that first year, Steve's business partner and I sold the Sheik's Property together, followed by the largest private home in Beverly Hills. The home was in such a poor state we ended up selling it for $13,000,000. That sounds like a lot of money, but when you consider it is still the largest private home in Beverly Hills, it really is not a lot of money. Upon selling the Sheik's Property and the biggest house in Beverly Hills, I was now on the map. Mind you, I was negotiating on the phone for these properties in my high school math class.

There are such contrasts between working in a small company versus a large company. When you work for a large company, you have the backing of a major name behind you, which really helps. Working for Steve, I had a very impressive brochure of a hundred $20,000,000 houses the company had sold, but this was over a fifty-year period. When going out for my own listings, I would call up Steve, he would get the old Bentley out of the garage and he would assist me on listing appointments. But after a while, I realized, this was not working. I really admire Steve, and am honored that I worked for him. To watch him show a property was just like experiencing a perfectly choreographed ballet. There was order, precision, and complete attention to detail. The adjective he used most was "perfection," everything was "gorgeous" and "fabulous" and "divine." Steve was incredibly talented; he really was one of the great salesmen of his time.

If he wrote a book, it would have been a best seller and that's what he should have done. He knew where all the bodies were buried. You could point to any property and he could tell you the history from A to Z. If you drive down the street with me today, because of the esoteric knowledge I picked up from Steve, I will tell you who lives where, what they paid for it and even how much they owe. I can truly say there are very few brokers who can do that, and clients love it. Another reason I am able to recite arcane details is that I started collecting books on the history of Beverly Hills and Hollywood when I was a little boy. This was a fascination I have always had, but Steve is the one who really taught me about the history of the homes of Beverly Hills. Ulti-

135

mately, I realized that I had to do things on my own. I decided that I was going to promote the hell out of myself and make a name for myself in the high-end residential market. The best way to tell you how I did what I did is to just tell you about my first listings.

I had graduated from high school and had my first taste of high-end residential real estate through Steve Meyers. It was time now to go out and get my own listings. Although it is illegal to "door knock" in the city of Beverly Hills and I would never do it today, I got my first listings that way, and these were not small listings. My first sale was of a house on Laurel Way. I saw a sign out front, which said "For Sale by Owner." I rang the bell, and a gentleman named Robert came out of the door and I convinced him to get me a meeting with the owner who was his best friend. I told this man that if he got me the listing, I would give him $50,000 upon the close of escrow on the house. Eager to get his $50,000, Robert was very helpful in the sales process and one month later I sold the house for an extraordinarily high price. I fetched $5,600,000 for a house, which was worth $4,500,000 on its best day. Since the house had been owned by a pseudo celebrity fifty years prior, I immediately called up Ruth Ryan of the *Los Angeles Times* and said, "Ruth, put this house in the *Hot Properties* section. It was owned by 1920's starlet Ruth Chatterton." She said, "Who is Ruth Chatterton?" I said, "I don't know, but I'm sure she was important at one time or another." I knew the importance of getting my name out there and I somehow convinced her to publish the property in the *Hot Properties* column of the *Los Angeles Times.*

One of the greatest things I have gained out of being involved in Beverly Hills real estate is an appreciation of the characters I have met. There is a difference between weird people and eccentric people. Weird people are those who you kind of want

136

to stay away from because they scare you and sometimes give you the vibe that they are really dangerous. Eccentric people are odd people, often with money, who can be very endearing. I like working with eccentric people. I have done business with many eccentric people, and most all of my experiences have been great. Truthfully, I think it is because I can relate to them.

Just after the sale of the Laurel Way property, a gentleman named Hank called me up off the Laurel "for sale" sign and inquired about the house. I told him the property was sold, but I knew of other properties I could show him. I met Hank, and I have to tell you, the guy looked like he was homeless. He was dressed very poorly and was driving a twenty-five-year-old Mercedes-Benz. Now, one thing my grandmother always taught me was to beware of the guy who drives up in the Bentley wearing a Rolex. It's the guy in the sweat pants and the old car who you want as your customer. Hank took me to lunch at Mr. Chow's and we got along really well. We looked at a few properties, and then a few more properties but none of them were right. We looked at house after house, and every house was almost perfect, but lacked something. In the meantime, he kept taking me to lunches and I thought to myself, "Hell, if he wants to take me to Spago two times a week and doesn't buy a house, that's fine by me." He was so strange. He would show up to these restaurants in sweat pants, and would order ten different items off of the menu and share everything. He would ask me what I wanted to eat, and before I could tell him, he would say to the waitress, "Okay let's have one of these, and one of these." He would spill his food everywhere and we would look at houses afterwards with spaghetti bolognese all over his pants. Hank also had a weird germ thing; he would never shake anyone's hand, but I still had faith in this guy.

Other brokers who knew I was working with him would call me and say, "You're wasting your time, he has been looking

137

for five years, and he's never going to buy anything. He has no money." I have been around money my entire life, and I smelled it. I knew this guy was the real deal. It didn't matter to me that he lived in a tiny shoebox in South Beverly Hills. I didn't doubt for a minute that this guy was the real deal. Now we had been into it for six months and before I knew it, I started walking with him and his cronies in their walking club. Hank, a doctor friend of his and another guy and I would walk around Holmby Park every afternoon and discuss properties. He would also tell me about his friends, many of whom I knew, and that helped me because I confirmed with them what I already knew about Hank, that he was very eccentric, completely unpretentious and had a lot of money to spend on a house. So one day, I called up one of my attorneys and said, "Ted, I'd like to show your house to a client of mine. Would you sell it for $10,000,000?" He said, "Josh, for ten million bucks, I would sell my wife." I showed Hank the house and he made an offer on it. Not only was it an offer, but it was a $9,000,000 all cash offer, which closed in one week. A week after closing on this gorgeous home in Bel Air, Hank tore it down! I told you, this guy was eccentric. The house was a designer show-place and he just tore it down. Now I had my second big sale in the bag.

The next deal I made was one of my favorites. One day, I rang the bell of a very famous Hollywood publicist named Mark. Mark was one of the great Hollywood publicists; he had managed so many A-list celebrities. As with everyone in Hollywood, when you reach a certain age, they throw you out, and Mark was no exception. Mark lived in a house on Beverly Crest Drive in Beverly Hills. At this time, I was renting a charming English Tudor house that once belonged to William Randolph Hearst and Marion Davies, on Readcrest Drive. I walked up to Mark's house and knocked on his door. Truthfully, I knocked on his door not because I thought he was going to sell his house, but because I had heard rumors that he had fallen on hard times, and I felt badly for the guy. He was so big at one time and now everyone had forgotten about him, so I thought, why not let him know there is still someone out there that remembers him.

I rang the bell and out came Mark. He was wearing a cowboy belt and some outrageous purple Louis Vuitton shoes. Mark was the most flamboyant man you could imagine. This guy was a character, and couldn't have been happier to talk to me. He invited me in and we talked for hours, smoking like chimneys on his balcony. We became fast friends. A few months later though, he died. He had a heart attack, and just like that, he was gone.

After Mark died, he didn't leave anything to his kids and whatever little money he still had, he left to his housekeeper, who was there by his side for thirty-five years. I called up his business manager and made a listing appointment. The business manager appreciated the fact that I had been friendly with Mark, so he gave me the listing. I sold the house within a month. Sadly, a developer tore it down and could not afford to build a new house when the market shifted. Unfortunately, the lot is still sitting there. A sad ending to a sad story.

So now that I was on a roll, I thought to myself, "How can I take this to the next level?" And I thought about the legendary brokers before me: Elaine Young, Thelma Orloff, and Mike Silverman. I thought about how the legendary Mike Silverman used to do swan dives into the pool of the Beverly Hills Hotel and emerge from the water with a laminated business card. I wanted to be just like him! I wanted to be an innovator and to be remembered as a legend in the industry. These brokers, all of them, were so extravagant and did everything outside of the box. I thought to myself,

139

"I've been outside of the box my entire life," and that's when I started to really step up my game.

If I did not make a career out of real estate, I should have gone into publicity. If there's one thing I've learned, it's that you need to really make a name for yourself. To do this you have to make your mark, and make it in a spectacular way. It's not the quantity of sales that create an image, it's the type of sales that you make. I do not do volume. I don't even want to do volume. I don't want to have a hundred listings and I don't want to work so hard that I can't enjoy my life. I want to be happy. Some of these "power brokers" work so hard that they have not been on a vacation in ten years. Some of them have never taken a vacation in their entire lives. I don't want to live that way.

This is the way my business is structured. On average, I make one sale a month, and I carry usually no more than three or four listings at a time. On average, the homes I sell are around $4,000,000 to $5,000,000. I "pop" two or three huge ones every year, and considering there are roughly ten homes a year that sell for over $10,000,000, I would say I am doing quite well. People have the misconception that every day another home sells for $10,000,000 or $20,000,000 in Beverly Hills. This is not the case. So I am not a volume broker, but I am a high numbers broker and that is why I earned the reputation of only selling the most expensive homes. As my former mentor Steve used to brag, "Only 35 homes have sold for over $10 million in the history of Beverly Hills and I have brokered ten of them." Now, I cannot say that I have sold ten of the thirty-five homes ever sold above ten million, but at twenty-five-years-old, I have already sold four of them, and in my opinion, that's not too bad.

As I said, I am not a volume broker. It is my opinion and firm belief that if you take on too many listings and deals, you cannot provide your clients with the service they expect. My clients expect a certain level of attention from me, and when you have ten or twenty listings at a time, there is no way to give them that attention. If I get more than ten listings, and between Beverly Hills and Orange County, I often do, I farm my listings out to other brokers that specialize in these areas and I co-list the properties with them. If I keep my inventory manageable, then my clients will like my service and use me again and refer me to their friends. I would rather have one hundred great repeat clients, than five hundred clients who don't ever want to use me again, but more importantly, will not refer me to their friends.

Many of the brokers out there hire a sales team. I will never, and I stress never, hire a team of agents to work under my name. There is only one person I genuinely trust to start and finish a transaction and avoid the pitfalls of real estate, and that's me. Maybe I'm not the ultimate high-end broker yet, but I know one thing, my clients know I am willing to go the distance to attain their goals. Many brokers that hire these teams come in for a listing appointment, and after that, the client never even sees him or her again. Showings are conducted by the sales team, escrow is handled by them, and everything else is handled by them. So what is the broker there for? When you hire these brokers, all you are doing is hiring their names. I tell everyone when I go on a listing appointment upfront, "You will not be dealing with a sales team or three assistants. You won't have to worry about not reaching me all day. You will have a direct number to me at all times and all showings will only be done by me." The most important part of my job is the showing of the properties and I can't stand the brokers that do not do showings. Having an assistant or an intern do your showings is, in my opinion, irresponsible. There is one lady I know, we will call her Tanya; she employees about half a dozen girls, all gorgeous blondes, and they do all the showings and handle all the transactions for her. Tanya probably doesn't even know her own clients' names. She is simply a figurehead.

I believe I possess a few qualities, which a broker must possess to be successful. First, I publicize myself every chance I get. Second, I really know how to show a property to its best advantage, and, third, I know how to finance a deal creatively and successfully, and finally, I know how to close deals. Let me explain all of these.

I have already discussed how important it is to publicize. When I started making money selling properties, I took all of that money plus more and reinvested it into advertising. I took out full-page ads in high-end publications. I contacted different media outlets and I milked my age as a story angle to get written up in the paper. I recall one article, the very first one, when I was in high school, which appeared in the *Beverly Hills Courier*, entitled "BH Student Set to Make Records," or something to that effect. Whenever I suggested story angles to papers, I would get chummy with the writers and I would say something like, "You know, why don't I save you some time. I know myself a lot better than you ever could. Instead of you writing about me and interviewing me and having to ask me a ton of questions, why don't I send you over a draft of a few things about myself that you might find interesting?" Within twenty-four hours, I had a well-written, self-promotional piece that could win a Pulitzer Prize. I knew how important this was for my career. So because of my age, I was smart enough to use this to my benefit. In fact people always used to ask me, "Does being so young hurt you?" Hurt me? It was the best thing that ever happened to me! It is the reason for my success. I think that people pay more attention to your achievements if you do them when you are young versus if you do them when you are older.

Just like Steve would have done absolutely anything for his clients in his heyday, there are no limits to what I will do for my clients. I think I must have been watching a movie one night at home and I vaguely remember seeing an episode of a TV show where someone was giving a tour of the city to someone else in a helicopter. I thought to myself, "I don't think a real estate agent has ever done that before." So before I knew it, I was chartering helicopters and showing my clients properties from the sky. And it worked. A Beverly Hills doctor called me one day from an ad he saw on a house I was selling, and he inquired about it. We discussed it and I showed it to him, but it wasn't his taste. I asked him what he was doing on Saturday and after he told me he had no plans, I asked him if he was afraid of flying.

There is no better way to see a property than from the sky. I didn't know what I was going to show him ahead of time. I just stuck my head out the window and when I saw a property that I thought he might like, I would point it out to him. I noticed one that had been on the market a few months earlier, but since the agent handling the property had died, I did not know who to get in touch with. So I made some phone calls and got to the U.S. Marshall's Office. Apparently the owner of the house was in jail for tax evasion, and the Marshall's Service was handling the sale of the property. I got them to let my client and me into the house and before I knew it he wrote an offer on the property. We closed escrow two weeks later. Those were in the days when a jackrabbit could get a loan on a property. All you needed was a pulse and the banks would extend you credit. This is definitely not the case today.

Before the advent of *Google Earth* another trick I had up my sleeve was that I would charter a helicopter, go up and start snapping photographs of any house I could. I would take four or five hundred pictures at a time and then I would knock on the doors

143

of four or five hundred houses, visit the owners and give them the aerial photographs as a gift. I would tell them who I was and that I thought they might like to have a photo of their property and should they ever want to sell their house, to call me. I sold a lot of houses that way. I would do these helicopter rounds until I hit every high-end property in town, and I now have a database of every major estate on the Westside. Should I get called up for a listing, nine times out of ten, I come prepared with a beautiful photograph taken by myself which really impresses the owner because I always tell them I went up the day before just to get them the photograph.

One time, I was in the middle of one of my helicopter flights and suddenly found that I had to go to the bathroom. There were no other options than returning to Burbank Airport and I wasn't about to schlep twenty minutes across town to pee. So I did what anyone else would do. I told the pilot to land the helicopter on an abandoned piece of land at the top of Tower Grove Drive in Beverly Hills. The property once belonged to the Shah of Iran, followed by Merv Griffin and then Mark Hughes. I got out of the helicopter, took a pee while being watched by a raccoon, got back into the helicopter and was on my way. Unfortunately for me, the F.A.A. found out and I was fined for landing a helicopter in Beverly Hills. Who knew you couldn't land a three-ton machine in the middle of Beverly Hills?

Going back to the importance of being a showman, ever since I was a little boy, I dreamed about one day building a home and surprising my wife with a house, and wrapping it in a big red bow. Well, things didn't turn out exactly as planned, but I never let go of my dream of wrapping a house in a big red bow. One day, my grandmother Edith called me over and told me one of her old friends, Elaine, had passed away. I have to say that my grandmother is an excellent source for business. She is ninety-

144

one and unfortunately many of her friends are dying. I don't want to be thought of as a death proprietor, however, someone is going to sell the house, so it may as well be me.

After Elaine died I went over to the house and met with her children. Well, as nice as Elaine was, I can't say the same about one of her daughters. To call her a bitch would be putting it mildly. Against my advice, the house was listed a million dollars over what I told her it was worth. I then got an offer of exactly what I told her the house would fetch. She pulled one on me and said, "I will not take this offer unless you cut your commission in half." Well, that wasn't about to happen, but then she pulled this card on me, "Well, if you don't cut your commission in half I won't take any offers from you and will use someone else to sell the house." So I thought to myself, "Should I do the right thing and tell her to go screw herself or should I just take half the money and run?" I took half the commission and called it a day, but I did promise myself that I would never take half a commission again. Upon the close of escrow, I tied the house in a big red bow and delivered the house to the clients. It made quite an impression and was photographed and put in the local paper. Of course, the paper did not get wind of it on their own; I called them up myself and told them to run a story. It was things like this that gave me a name around town.

My next sale was a good one. A high school friend of mine told me her parents were interested in buying a new house and said if I could find them something spectacular, they would consider moving. They really were not serious about buying, but if something really special came up, they would look into it. I kept this in the back of my mind and a few months later, I looked at a house on Foothill in Beverly Hills and immediately knew it was perfect for them. I took my friend's parents over, and they loved it, but of course, they did not show that they loved it right

145

away. They played hardball and pretended they were not interested, but if they could get the house for a steal, they would buy it. I was onto my client's game though and I knew they loved the house. The sellers were asking $15,000,000 and my buyers were at $12,000,000. Somehow, I negotiated them up to $13,500,000 and we had a deal. The sellers were upset because they didn't think they got enough for the house, and even though the house in today's market is only worth $9,000,000, the sellers have still not thanked me for getting them a record price on their street. After my clients moved in, they asked me to sell their old house, and I sold it off the market for $10,000,000.

There's an expression that "buyers are liars" because what they say when they are buying something and what they say when they are selling something are two completely different things. When I sold this house to my clients for $13,500,000, the buyer kept saying to me he would not go up or budge even $100,000. He kept telling me that he thought he was paying a premium for the house and he was not going to pay a penny more. Well, we came to a standstill because the seller was not going to come down $100,000 and the buyer was not going to come up $100,000. I told the other broker to kick in $50,000 and I would kick in $50,000 and we would make a deal. It was worth it because we each had a quarter of a million dollars in commissions on the table. So, we made the deal.

About a month after we closed escrow, I got a call from my client, the new owner of the property. He said to me, "Josh, you know I got a very good deal on my house, it is two acres in prime Beverly Hills. If you come across someone who wants to pay $20,000,000 I would consider selling it, but I won't take anything less." I said to him, "Bob, that's amazing, a month ago you were overpaying for the house at $13,500,000, and now you won't accept anything less than $20,000,000!" The other thing I found interesting is that when I sold him the house, it was one acre, but a month later, it grew to be two acres. Buyers really can be liars!

Now I was on a roll, and there was nothing stopping me. The next house I brokered was the biggest one I ever sold and still holds a record as being the most expensive house sold south of Lexington Road in Beverly Hills. I sold the house for $25,000,000. I cannot talk about this one because everything was confidential, however I can assure you, I was quite pleased. Although there were four brokers involved, everyone went home happy. Later on that year, I also sold a $3,500,000 tear down on Rexford Drive in Beverly Hills, a $3,000,000 home on Trousdale Place as well as a $4,500,000 house on Martin Lane in Trousdale Estates. I also leased a house to a media mogul, who as wealthy as he is only leases houses, and does not buy them. I leased him a home for $50,000 a month in Beverly Hills and the reason this was such an interesting deal was because it was my friend's house. My friend, Stanton, had just passed away from cancer. He was a longtime client of mine and he was my lunch buddy. In fact, a month before he died, we came very close to buying a second home for him in Beverly Hills. Stanton spent a good five years building his masterpiece in Beverly Hills. When I say this is a masterpiece, I would consider this one of the finest homes I have ever seen. After Stanton died unexpectedly, his brother asked me to lease out the house. I brought the media mogul up to see it, and worked a deal with him. It always makes me proud when I represent a property and I represent a buyer. But it is very hard when you have to sell a friend's house that has just passed away.

You know, in real estate, there is a distinct difference between buyers and sellers and to be a really good broker, you have to know how to work with both of them. This is what makes the difference between a good broker and a great broker. A good broker can sell a house to a client, but a great broker can sell a house to a client and then resell it shortly thereafter, which brings to mind my favorite deal that I have ever made.

I got a call one day from an associate of mine, Brendan. I had met him in a club in Hollywood about a year earlier and he told me he wanted to get into the business. I told him to call me when he got his license, never thinking I would hear from him again. Lo and behold, I got a call from him a year later, and I appreciated his tenacity. Most prospective realtors say, "I want to get into real estate," but they never follow up. This guy really showed that he cared and he wanted to learn from me. I was by now, seasoned enough that I could teach him a thing or two.

Brendan called when I was staying at the Dorchester in London. He said to me, "I got us a client." I said "That's great, tell me about him." So Brendan said, "A gentleman by the name of Lord Chesterfield called me from Barbados and said he wants to buy a $10,000,000 house, all cash, in Beverly Hills." I immediately started laughing because nobody ever calls up and says, "I want to buy a ten million dollar house all cash. It just sounded too funny for me to believe. I left London and flew back to Beverly Hills. Brendan told me that Lord Chesterfield was supposedly checking into the Beverly Hills Hotel in two days and wanted to see properties right away. So I said to Brendan, let me do a little investigating.

I was friendly with the general manager of the Dorchester in London. Being the parent hotel of The Beverly Hills Hotel, I called up the GM and asked him to find out if a Lord Chesterfield was going to be checking into the Beverly Hills Hotel in a few days.

My manager friend said, "Do you mean Arthur Chesterfield?"

I said, "Yes, do you know him?"

He said, "Know him? He is one of the best clients of the Dorchester Collection. He always stays in the Presidential suite of our hotel."

I thanked him and knew Brendan and I were in business. Brendan and I went to the Beverly Hills Hotel to pick up Lord Chesterfield for our showings. We greeted him in the lobby and found him to be very reserved and very proper, and he came prepared with newspapers full of homes he wanted to see. I do not know how it happened, but we really hit it off and by lunchtime, Brendan, Lord Chesterfield, his wife and I were at Geoffrey's in Malibu for lunch. He was a blast, but he had a temper and, let's just say, you did not want to get on his bad side.

We must have seen ten different homes all over ten million dollars in a matter of three days. On the third day, we saw our final house on the list and if he didn't like this one, that was it, there were no other houses to show him. He even mentioned to us that if he did not find anything, he would just look somewhere else in the United States, possibly Arizona or Texas. I thought to myself, "I don't know anything about Arizona, think quick." Sure enough, I showed him the final house on my list, and he did not like it. Just as he was about to thank us for our time and tell us he was going to look elsewhere, I thought of something.

I called up a broker friend of mine and I asked him if he could get me into a house that was just about to come on the market in Brentwood Park. I took Lord Chesterfield to the house. The owner was asking $16,000,000 for the house. This was when the market was still good, but was just about to take a turn for the worse. Lord Chesterfield walked in and said, "I will pay $13,000,000." Relieved that we finally found a house he liked, I was also nervous because I knew the seller would never take $13,000,000. I told Lord Chesterfield to make it $14,000,000 and he unwillingly

149

obliged. Long story short, we made a deal. We closed escrow in three days, and it was probably the fastest $14,000,000 escrow in the history of Los Angeles. The money was wired from Barbados, we made the record sale for a house in Brentwood Park and that was that, or so I thought.

Lord Chesterfield didn't know anyone here, he was moving to California because he liked the weather. I took his wife to Brentwood Country Club for lunch in hopes that if she liked it, my parents could perhaps sponsor them and help get them acquainted with people. But that was not necessary. Lord Chesterfield decided within a matter of months he wanted a bigger property and he wanted to sell the Brentwood Park house. Brendan and I were more than happy to accommodate him.

I was in the process of a minor cosmetic surgery and I was heavily sedated on morphine at the time. I was in an outpatient center in Santa Monica when I got a call from a voice, which sounded vaguely familiar to me.

"Josh, Chesterfield wants to dump the house and get a bigger pad," said the voice.

I said, "Fabulous. Who is Chesterfield and who are you?"

He said, "Josh, it's Brendan! Lord Chesterfield wants to sell the house in Brentwood!"

After a few rounds of this, the medication was slowly wearing off and I realized where I was. A few days later, we put the house on the market for $17,000,000 and sold the home for $14,500,000 within a month. Not only was this a huge sale, but we broke our first record and still hold the record for the highest sale in Brentwood Park. The market had just turned and prices were now falling. I did not think there was a chance Chesterfield was going to

get out of this house without losing money. But I was so wrong.
A wealthy man from Mexico, and probably the only man in the
universe who would ever pay $14,500,000 for this house came by
and made an offer of $14,200,000. Chesterfield refused to lose a
nickel, and since there were commissions to be paid, the buyer's
broker and I cut a deal and we all went home happy. Brendan
and I threw in $100,000 together and the buyer's agent threw in
$100,000.

The buyer noticed that Chesterfield owned a limited edition
of a book, which was on the shelf of the library. Thinking he was
kidding, the buyer said he would buy the house only if the book
was thrown in the deal. Not thinking anything of it, I said to
the guy "If you buy the house, the book is yours." The book was
entitled *Good Meat* and not knowing the sentimental value it had
to the owner, I did not think it would be an issue.

Chesterfield said, "No way, cancel the deal. I'm not giving him
my *Good Meat* book."

We were a few days short of closing escrow and I didn't know
what to do. The buyer was very upset and threatened to cancel
the deal if he didn't get the *Good Meat* book. Brendan and I
were at a loss, so we offered the buyer $25,000 to forget about the
damn book. And that was that, or so I thought. The kicker is that
the buyer then put the house on the market six months after they
moved in because they thought there were ghosts. They put it on
for $13,000,000 and can't even get $10,000,000 for it today. If it
sells, it will have changed hands five times in the last three years.
Maybe it really does have ghosts! The final chapter to this transaction is that Chesterfield bought a ten-acre property because
he wanted more room. He decided it was too far from his kid's
school and I now have that house on the market!

Never write people off in life because you never know when they are going to call you to buy a house. When I was in high school, I started talking to a boy online...I know, real classy. Mind you, these were still in the days when it was not that easy to meet a guy your own age and go on a date. It's amazing how much things have progressed just in the last ten years. Well, after talking with the boy for a while, it turned out that I knew his family. The problem was this boy was not out of the closet and he was petrified I was going to tell his parents. I assured him I was not like that, and that I wanted to meet him for dinner. We met for dinner, and I liked the guy's personality, but there was really nothing there in terms of pursuing a relationship. We never spoke again after that dinner.

About five years later, I was having dinner and I bumped into him and he knew I never said anything to anyone, so he trusted me. He said he was looking for a house and I ended up selling him one for $2,000,000. The moral of the story is: don't betray people's trust and they will respect you. In fact, I was even invited to his engagement party to his new wife. Boy is he going to have some explaining to do later in life.

Now, I don't want you to think real estate has been all fun and up periods for me. Believe me, I have had my share of downs. I know thus far it sounds like I had a smooth ride to the top, but let me tell you, it's been like driving an old Rolls Royce. The car looks beautiful on the outside, but it's in the shop every five minutes. For everything good that happened to me in my career, I would say I had just as much bad luck. For everything negative that has happened to me, I learned from it, and it made me that much better of an agent. As you go, you learn along the way, hoping to offend as few people as possible throughout the journey. You learn from your mistakes, and I have made plenty of them. I still make mistakes because in six years, you can't be expected to know everything. For one, I had a giant ego, two, I was overly aggressive and three, I felt that I was invincible. I must say that sometimes these things worked in my favor, but in many more instances they hurt me.

If you're a young guy, and you start making a bunch of big deals, and you are working with a group of brokers who are much older than you, my advice now would be to lay low and not rub it in their faces. Yes, it feels great to know you are doing such big things at such a young age, and yes you want to let the whole world know, but the world will find out on its own and ultimately it's better not to talk about it. You only create enemies that way and because I was so open about my successes, I created a lot of enemies. I never did anything wrong to these people, but they resented me. That is my biggest regret and I pay for it every day.

Now that I have mentioned what I did wrong and what I would have done differently if I could change things, let me now tell you about the things that were not within my control, and still went wrong. These are the things that happened because of my lack of experience and because of bad luck.

In this world, there are stupid people, and then there are really stupid people. One of the dumbest people that I ever worked with was a gentleman named...well let's just call him Tom. I took Tom to see a property on Hillcrest Drive in Beverly Hills that was not yet on the market and had belonged to a friend of my grandmother. So, I take him to see the house on Hillcrest Drive, and he falls in love with the property. We write up an offer and I submit it to the sellers. At some point during the transaction, Tom thought it would be cute to go directly to the seller and try and negotiate a deal without me. Tom told me that he had lost interest in the house and I believed him, so I stopped working on the house for him. He purchased the house without my knowledge.

153

I found out about it a month later when I was going through the tax rolls. I took him to court and the arbitrator immediately ruled in my favor. I won a judgment against him. Sounds like a happy ending to an ugly story, right? The only problem is he killed himself later. My luck, the bastard couldn't pay me my money before he decided to "check out."

When you first get into the business, your priorities are different. You will take any listing regardless of what price it is and regardless of whether you can or cannot sell it, simply because you want to get your name out there. In many ways, it can be a good practice. I took a lot of overpriced listings in the beginning of my career because I thought it was important to associate my name with high-end estates. As time went on though, I was able to pick and choose listings, and no longer needed to do this. In the beginning, I was so eager to get my foot in the door that I did the same with buyers. Heck, if you came up to me at the Coffee Bean and Tea Leaf, and said you wanted to buy a $20,000,000 house, I would have started showing you properties. It was because I did not have the knowledge at the time, to realize that people will take advantage of you and people will tell you they want to look at expensive homes just because they have never seen an expensive home before.

This reminds me of an agent I know who one time showed some clients a house on the beach for ten million dollars. They kept raving about how much they loved the house during the entire showing and by the end, the agent asked the clients if they were going to make an offer. The clients responded, "Well we would if we could afford it, we are waiting until we get our money." The agent said, "What do you mean?" The clients simply responded, "We are playing the lottery very actively every day and we know we are going to win soon." People are crazy! There was another gentleman whose home I listed once in Bel Air. I thought

154

just because he could afford to pay for my dinner at L'Orangerie, this guy was legitimate. It never even crossed my mind to pull the title on his property before I listed it. He even gave me stock in his company! I listed his property and a few days later he was arrested and is now serving a thirty-year stint at Lompoc Prison.

When I first got into the business, I thought it would be a great idea to take out monthly ads in a very popular weekly paper in Beverly Hills. I was promised the cover of the magazine if I advertised with them for a year, but never got anything in writing. A year came and went and so did $25,000 of my advertising money. They never gave me my magazine cover. They asked me to advertise with them for another year and they would consider a cover for me, obviously I told them to take a hike.

I have also made some really costly mistakes. Here's a perfect example of how lack of experience did me in. There was a gentleman, let's just call him Mick, who was developing a huge house in Beverly Hills. Eager to get his listings, I approached him and told him I was the best broker in town to sell his property. Everything seemed to be going really smoothly and just as we were about to sign the contracts, he asked me if I wanted to joint venture with him on a property in Palm Springs. Because I wanted his Beverly Hills listing so badly, it was difficult for me to say no, so I agreed to look at it. Mick convinced me that we were going to make millions together on this property and I ended up giving him $250,000.

I now had the listing on his Beverly Hills house. When I was going to list it originally, I thought he was going to be a realistic seller and list the property at around $9,000,000. The day we finalized the papers, he told me he thought it should be listed at $16,000,000. Contrary to my advice, he insisted and now we had a ridiculous listing for $16,000,000 on the market. We all know

155

the biggest curse for a property is to overprice it. The market started to fall and so did the value of the house. By the third reduction, Mick was convinced the house wasn't selling because of my lack of marketing abilities. He refused to admit that the house had originally been listed at the wrong number and at this point the whole real estate business took a nosedive. He decided to pull the listing away from me, and you can imagine the rest of the story. The market in Palm Springs crashed and to this day, I'm stuck with three pieces of dirt worth maybe a tenth of what I paid for them. If you ever need a place to stay in Palm Springs, I have a lovely lot on the corner of Avenida Cerca and the main highway. You're more than welcome to pitch a tent there and stay the evening. The utilities are very low because there are none.

One day, I was doing an open house in Beverly Hills and in walked a well-known celebrity who will remain nameless. I got a little friendly with him. While he was actually quite a nice guy, he and his advisor would show up late to appointments, not call to tell me they were late and make me wait for hours. I took them to lunch at Hillcrest Country Club with my family, and never got a thank you. However, the worst situation was when I showed him a house, and he bought it through another broker behind my back. To make matters worse, the house belonged to my parents' best friends. Double commission lost. That wasn't the first time nor will it be the last time that I have been suckered.

Here is another one. I knew a woman who wanted to sell her house in Beverly Hills. Before we were about to put the house on the market, she wanted to find another house. So I took this woman out to see houses, and we saw everything. We looked at house after house, and then she started liking some houses, and started making offers, and the offers were accepted and we were in escrow. We went in and out of six escrows on different properties. With every different property, she found a problem.

156

She smelled mold, she thought the windows were not properly sealed, or that the home's feng shui was off. Every time we did an inspection, she would find the smallest thing and make an issue out of it. The sellers were usually willing to work with her because her offers were really very solid, but by the time the inspections were done, she was asking the sellers to practically rebuild the house. I finally had enough and told her off. This was the one time I ever told a client off, but I truthfully felt at this point she was using me and she was screwing around. Her behavior was so erratic and her moods would change so frequently, I couldn't take it any longer and I blew up. I wrote her a very nasty e-mail, which again, I shouldn't have done. She responded with some ridiculous metaphor about a tiger and an ox and about life lessons and youth, and frankly I just didn't care. A month later, she bought one of the houses I showed her for $7,000,000 and e-mailed me something about Buddha. I was so angry. The lesson I learned, though, was never to tell a client off, even if they are in the wrong. If you don't want to work with someone anymore, just simply say, "I don't think this is working out and I want the best for you. I am going to refer you to someone else."

There was another woman I worked with once. She had been calling me off and on for two years and she always wanted me to invite her to parties and to different events. I actually did invite her to some different things because I felt badly for her and she had a $2,000,000 house to sell, so I thought, even if she is not ready right now, in the future she will use my services. When she finally was ready to sell her house, she asked me over to sign the papers. Just as we were about to sign the documents, she pulled out a bill to fix her computer for $2,000.

I said, "What is this?"

She said, "Well, before I sell my house I need to test how far you are willing to go for me, I need a broker who is going to do things for me."

When I know something is wrong, and my gut tells me there is a problem, I go with it. I knew this woman was not going to sell her house, I knew she was not a realistic seller and after losing three quarters of a million dollars with the guy in Palm Springs, I wasn't in any mood to fork over another $2,000 to help this charity case.

I said, "I am not going to pay your computer bill, but I will tell you what I will do. If I sell the house, I will give you $2,000, and you have my word on that and I will gladly put it in writing."

She said, "No, I need to test you right now."

I knew the woman was having some financial problems, and maybe I could have sold her house and made a lot of money on the commission, but frankly I was not about to pay this woman's bill to fix her computer. Sometimes, you have to go with principle and do what is right, even if it may not be the best financial decision.

I'll tell you another cute little story. Some friends of my grandparents fell upon financial problems in the 90's. Being the kind of people my grandparents were, they gave the husband and wife jobs at the Flagg Building on Beverly Drive. My grandparents knew that it would be less demeaning than to just hand over some money to them, so my grandfather created jobs for them. He really did not need them at all, but he wanted to help them. They ended up getting back on their feet and actually became quite wealthy. They both died and it did not even cross my mind for a second that the children would not give me the listing on their house. After all, my family had been very kind to them. I called them, and they never called me back. My grandmother shared the same secretary with them, so I asked the secretary if the kids were in town. She told me they were, so I was surprised I did not hear back from them. I called again, and nothing. Finally on the third time, I happened to reach them. The son who was running the estate for his parents said, "Sorry I didn't have time to get back to you, I have been really busy. Anyway, we just gave the listing to someone who specializes in the Wilshire Corridor." I did not say anything because I knew my grandmother would be upset, but I thought to myself, "You creep." My grandmother was appalled, but she was happy I did not open my mouth like I have been known to do. The lesson here is that with anything in life, you can never be sure how people will respond to any given situation.

These are just a few gems from my real estate journey. You all know there are tremendous highs, but there are equally tremendous lows. Staying in this business takes tenacity and a very thick skin. Real estate is a real love hate relationship. I love this business, but of course I hate it because of the long down times. Real estate is your mistress and you just have to stick with it until she's back in the mood to play.

In 2007, I left Steve Myers and went to work for a larger company. I worked there for a year, and then was offered a very good position at Keller Williams, where I still am to this day.

159

How to be a Successful Agent, Josh Flagg Style

Have a Group of Friends that Know what is going On

In the real estate business, to be successful, you have to have a group of friends who are really savvy and are really good at what they do. They have to have a genuine interest in real estate and have great connections in the industry. This is your group that you exchange information with. To keep up with the group you are always going to have to reciprocate and exchange information. In my business, I have a group of four or five guys that know what is going on at all times, and we constantly exchange information with each other. We know what houses are pocket listings, we know who is in escrow on certain properties, and we know what's going on behind the doors. This is a very valuable tool because being in the "know" is key to our business.

Do Not Take Anything Personally

You cannot take this business too personally. If you do, you will just get upset. There are so many times when I know I was responsible for a sale but did not get the commission. I have given out information to people in trust and confidence only to discover that they have taken that information to purchase a property without me. You cannot look back because it will just make you angry.

If you get screwed, just move on. The worst feeling in the world is when you know the seller of a property, you tell someone else about this property, and then they go behind your back and sell it. It happens all the time and when you are a third generation Los Angeleno and know a lot of people, it is a hard thing to avoid. I used to get depressed when this happened, but now I just think, "onwards and upwards."

Be Your Own Publicist

The words "publicist" and "real estate agent" should not be in the same sentence together. Forget about them; only you can be your own publicist because no one has your best interests at heart more than you do. When I say publicize yourself, it is great to get your name out there, but I am of the school of thought that it is better to be visible in the right places rather than just sticking your name anywhere. For instance, when I go to the grocery store and I see a picture of a real estate agent holding her dog on the shopping cart, I crack up laughing, or when I see an advertisement for a broker team at the car wash, I think to myself, "What, you can only find clients at the car wash?" Now, this is just my opinion, but I think it is important to put your name in the right places.

It's a great idea to send notepads out to houses in an area you want to serve because people always use paper. It's also a great idea to do mailings with homes that you have sold or currently have listed. I am a believer in that type of marketing. Putting your picture on a bus bench or on a shopping cart, especially in the high-end residential real estate market, while it is good exposure, I believe it diminishes your reputation. In lower end areas, it might not be such a bad idea, but if you want to sell homes over a million dollars, I think you should be very careful where you advertise.

Another great place to advertise, if it is affordable, is in your local newspaper. For instance if you are an agent in Beverly Hills, advertise in the *Beverly Hills Courier* where women reading the paper while getting their hair done will see you. That is great exposure. Not everyone reads the real estate section, so advertise where people look, regardless of whether they are in the market to buy or sell their home.

Only Make Personal Recommendations

If a client asks you to refer them to someone, for example, they want a great florist for a party, don't recommend a florist to anyone unless you or your closest friends have used that florist before. If someone asks you for a contractor, recommend someone you know who is really an upstanding human being. Making a recommendation of someone you are not one hundred percent sure about can be a huge mistake because when that person screws up, guess who is going to look like the idiot? You!

Be Careful with Commissions

When you are going up for a listing appointment and it's time to talk commissions, you better believe that eight out of ten times, the seller is going to try and cut down the commission. There is

163

nothing wrong or unusual about that, but you have to be careful. If you get in the habit of agreeing to take really low commissions, you will get that reputation.

Whenever I meet with a client and they say, "I want to cut your commission down from 2.5% to 1.5%," I always say flat out, "No." I then follow up with "If you want a 1% broker or a 1.5% broker, then I can refer you to someone who will put your house in the Multiple Listing Service and wait for it to sell itself. But if you want someone who is going to get you the highest price and work for the money, then go with a broker like me."

Be prepared to give a little discount if it makes the seller happy, but do not take listings for nothing. If at the last minute the buyer or the seller threatens to cancel if he does not get a credit, do not give anything away from your own commission. No one fails to buy a house they really want just because they need some extra money from their agent. Often sellers or buyers try to make a quick buck and get some money out of their agents at the end of the escrow. Respectfully tell them, that if the house is not for them, maybe they should consider a different property. They will buy the property and you won't walk away empty handed.

Don't Just Tell the Sellers What they Want to Hear

When you are pitching a listing, it is so important to be clear and upfront from the beginning or it is going to hurt you at the end of the transaction. Do not tell the seller what they want to hear; tell them the truth. Let's say you are going up on a listing, which is worth $4,000,000, and because you want to get the listing over the other competing brokers, you tell the seller you think it is worth $5,000,000. This is a big mistake, and I'll explain

164

why. There is a fifty percent chance the seller is going to list with you because you told him the house was worth more than anyone else, but what happens when you can't sell the house for that price? Who is going to get the blame? You are. The other problem with this is that if you tell someone his house is worth $5,000,000 when every other broker has told him or her that the house is worth $4,000,000, they are not going to trust you.

Tell them the truth and it is important to follow up with this statement: "The most important time for a listing is during the first few weeks it hits the market. This is a critical time when the limelight is on your house. If you are overpriced, the house will be overlooked and will be forgotten and you will then have to play the price reduction game where you are just dropping the price every month."

I don't care if it is an up market or a down market, but especially in a down market, it is important to price a house for what it is worth, or even a hair below, to build up the excitement. If you play your cards right, you will get multiple offers. If a house is worth $2,000,000, put it out for $2,000,000. You will either get full asking or you will sell it for over $2,000,000. If a house is worth $2,000,000 and you list it for $3,00,000 (especially in a down market) you will end up selling it for $1,500,000. Overpricing a property is the worst thing you can do, and the more days the house sits on the market, the less desirable the listing is and the staler the listing becomes.

The other thing to keep in mind is that if you tell the seller the truth about what his house is worth, and he does list the house with another broker who tells him his house is worth more, when the house does not sell and it expires from the market, the seller will call you and ask you to represent him on the second round.

Be a Control Freak

I am a control freak and with good reason. Don't be afraid to be the next Stanley Kubrick. You know what you want; you have a vision—go for it and do not let anyone interfere with it. When I have someone build a website for me, for instance, you better believe they want to quit after the first day because to them it is just another job, but to me, they are creating my calling card.

I am selling a lifestyle, not just a house, so I take what I do very seriously. Don't be afraid to be in control of your employees or people you hire. If you are paying for it, then you are entitled to have whatever you want done. Just always be polite and respectful even if you can tell your employee is getting irritated and tired. It may cost you more, but it always pays off in the end.

Never Put Anything in Writing that can come back to Bite You

Always remember that whatever you put in writing can come back to bite you. An e-mail you cavalierly wrote doesn't just disappear in the virtual atmosphere. Don't leave messages on phone machines that can come back to haunt you.

It is inevitable that you are going to say something negative about someone at some point during your career, and you better hope you are smart enough not to let someone have a record of it.

Always Qualify your Clients

Before you start showing properties, the most important thing you can do is to qualify the person you are showing properties to.

166

As I mentioned before, when I first got in the business I was eager to have anyone as my client so long as they had a pulse. The most important thing you can do as a good agent though is to qualify your buyers ahead of time.

Today, I get continuous calls from people who want to go out looking at houses. If I know the people or have done a deal with them, or if they have been referred by a personal relationship of mine it is one thing. However, if I cannot Google the individual, if I have never heard of the person, or if they call me out of the blue, you better believe the first thing I ask them for after, "How many bedrooms do you want?" is, "How much money do you have?" Maybe not so bluntly, but I will not start working with someone until I can qualify them as a legitimate buyer.

Do Not Harass Clients

If someone does not bother calling you back the first time, give him or her one more ring, it is possible they misplaced the message or the phone number. Everyone is guilty of it once in a while. If you call a second time, and they still do not call you back, don't call again, they don't want to buy the house and you are only making a fool of yourself.

I now know how annoying it is when people call you over and over. Recently, I got three calls from a brokerage house in New York. They wanted my business and I simply was not interested. I had never heard of them, but that's beside the point. The first time I was gracious and told them I would call them back because I was in a meeting. The second time I told them I was not interested but I would keep their number for future reference. The third time, I had to tell them that I was not interested in doing business with them at all.

Use Discretion when Picking a Brokerage to Work For

Do not go to a real estate company based on what you think they are going to do for you. When applying for jobs, get a written confirmation of what the company will pay for, what they will not pay for, what added fees there are, what advertising costs they will pick up, etc. Do not rely on what the broker tells you in your meeting with them because believe me, if it is not in writing, it doesn't mean anything.

Before I was at Keller Williams, I worked for an international real estate firm. I was told that I would be reimbursed for an ad I took out in the *Los Angeles Times*, which cost $2000. I did not even think it would be an issue.

I came to my broker to ask for my check one day and he said, "Corporate does not want to pay for it."

I said, "You told me the company would pay for it."

He said, "Sorry there is nothing I can do about it. I thought they would pay for it." So I left, and I did not stay much longer with that company.

Become Politically Active in Your Community

It is very important to become politically active in your community, and that is just what I did in 2006. My dear friend, was running for Beverly Hills City Council and I decided to help campaign for her. I did this because I thought she was a strong candidate and I liked her as a person. I threw a breakfast for her at the Beverly Hills Hotel and invited people to come hear her speak.

This was not just some ploy to meet people and earn business; it solidified my relationship with the woman who would soon become the Mayor of Beverly Hills, and believe me, it never hurts to be in tight with the powers that be.

Don't Trust Your Competition
...After All, They are Your Competition

Don't trust what brokers tell you because they are not genuinely your friends, They have one thing in mind, making money. When all is said and done, you are both after the same buyers. Do not believe what they say without fact checking first because they may be trying to throw you a fast one. As I mentioned before, it is very important to have a group of friends in your business that you can really trust. Know who your friends are and know who your enemies are, and keep your enemies as far away as possible.

Competition is healthy and you are entitled to make your pitch when you go up for a listing, but don't bad mouth your competition because it will only get back to them and it will make the client think you are threatened by other agents. The things I overhear some agents say about me when going up for a listing are inconceivable.

"He doesn't know how to sell a house."

"He gets all his listings from his family."

I can go on and on, I have heard it all. The bulk of everything is not only false, but such a fabrication of the truth, that it often makes me laugh.

Let me tell you one quick little anecdote about a broker who I considered to be a friend, until he really screwed me over. I was doing a probate sale and I was working with a cooperating broker, let's just call him Fred. The sale was a probate and because of an error on my brokers part, and the stupidity of the lawyers handling the deal, there was a box that was not checked in the contract, and what this little box did, was entitle whoever the first broker who brought an offer on the property, to a commission regardless of whether he sold it or not. We went to probate court, the house was sold to someone completely unrelated to the transaction, and to my dismay, I found out that I had to split my commission with two other brokers, one who deserved a commission, and one who did not. This broker, did not even realize this error himself and was surprised when escrow sent a check to his office of $40,000. $40,000 of my money. I called him up, and said, "Fred, you know there was an error in the contract and I am sure I don't have to tell you this, I know you are a good person and will do the right thing, can you please wire that money back to me?" He said, "I couldn't believe it when I got this money, I know I didn't sell it." I said "I know, crazy huh? Would you be kind enough to wire the money into my account at your convenience." He said, "Well Josh, you know, I really needed a new car and the money is spent already, I bought myself a car today." I said "Fred, that money is not yours, it was a clerical error in a contract and you did not deserve a commission on the sale." He did not care and that was that. There was nothing I could do, it was in writing, I had to just move on, but believe me, whenever I see him driving around in his Mercedes, I think to myself, "I hope he enjoys that car, because I bought it for him."

Sell a Property as Though You Were the Buyer

If you have taste and understand property value, it is a match made in heaven. Now, onto showing properties. If I learned anything from the person I started out in business with, it was how to show a property When I take someone into a house, I don't make him or her feel like it is my job to sell it to them. I take them in, and make them feel like I really want to be there because I honestly do. I proceed to show them the property and highlight the things that impress me the most. I show them how proud I am to be showing the house and they can feel it when I show it to them.

When the potential buyers talk to me about price, I say, "Look, if you don't buy it, someone else will and they are going to love it. If this isn't for you, let me recommend a few other houses which I think might be up your alley."

I then mention a few good houses, but none that are as good as the house I am showing them, and I compare and contrast with the buyer. I often say "Look, I am going to sell this regardless and I am not going to pressure you, only you can decide for yourself, but at least let me show you what this has to offer and show you why if I was in the market to buy a home right now, this would be the house I would consider."

Truthfully, it is hard to do this if you don't really believe in the house. If you actually believe in the house, you will be able to sell it very easily

I was doing a tour of a backyard once and was taking the buyers to the pool house. As if out of a movie, I walked a little too close to the edge of the pool and I fell in. I got right out of the pool, slipped on the homeowners robe and continued the show-

171

ing. I guess I really made quite a splash because the potential buyers did buy the house. When they asked me how deep the pool was, they were confident I wasn't lying to them. When we closed escrow, they sent me a pair of swim trunks as a gift.

When you Don't Know What to Do, Ring Someone's Bell

The best way to meet people in the real estate business is by ringing their doorbell. I remember one woman in particular named Gloria. This woman was fabulous and she knew my grandmother Margie. She had the most gorgeous house on north Beverly Drive. I drove up her driveway one day, and rang her bell, and this woman who looked like she was out of the movie *Sunset Boulevard* opened the door. She invited me in and it was like entering a time warp, but I felt comfortable there because it was the kind of stuff my grandparents had in their houses. It was the most beautiful house. When she passed away, her kids took care of the estate and gave the listing on the house to a friend that was a broker. They didn't have any idea that I was actually a friend of their mom's and used to go to the Bel Air Hotel for Bellinis with her. It doesn't matter though, I wouldn't trade the memories for anything!

There's nothing I like more than sitting and talking to older people. I am an old soul and I love hearing old stories and hanging out with older people because I just feel more comfortable with them. There was that one time at Mr. Grossman's house though, that even I could not listen any longer. The guy was so senile, he had me in the living room of his house for close to four hours looking through old pictures of him in the army. All he kept saying was "Who is that good looking guy in the picture there? Do you know who that is? Wasn't I a good looking guy?"

All I could keep saying for four hours was "You sure were the ladies man." The guy was really nice, but I could not listen to him ever again, so I never visited with Mr. Grossman again.

Don't Be Sure of Anything

When I first got in the business, I was sure of everything.

I would think to myself, "Oh, we're friends, I will for sure get the listing on her house, or, "Oh, I have known them for years, a hand shake is just fine, we don't need to sign that paper," or, "Oh, they would never sell their house with anyone else but me, I have been friends with their children for ten years."

Let me tell you. You can't be sure of anything in the real estate business. When you are dealing in numbers that are this high, people will do whatever is most beneficial for their pocket book. One of my own best friends bought a house without me. My own best friend! And that was after showing him homes for over two years.

Opening the Escrow is Just the First Step; Closing is What's Important

If you can't close a deal, nothing you're reading right now will matter. Be prepared for anything. In deals, things always come up at the last minute and you have to be willing to predict them ahead of time. If you are brokering a deal, put yourself in the shoes of whomever you are representing. Pretend you are buying the house for yourself and imagine what expectations you would have from the seller. Or, if you are representing the seller, imagine

173

that it's your home and you want to be protected and want it to be in the best shape possible. Pretend it is your house and expect from the buyer and the buyer's agent whatever you would expect.

In every deal, problems come up. The buyer wants a credit, the seller doesn't want to give it to him, the seller wants to take a chandelier with him, and the contract does not mention the chandelier. The buyer wants to renegotiate, the seller gets temperamental. Issues arise, and the slightest thing can tip the scale. Don't get overly emotional. Everything will work itself out.

Be an Innovator

Probably the most famous dirt peddler in Beverly Hills was a man by the name of Mike Silverman. Mike Silverman, while definitely not the first salesman in Beverly Hills, was by far the most famous. I believe because of his innovative style he will be talked about and remembered forever.

As mentioned earlier in the book, Mike Silverman was known for his swan dives into the pool of the Beverly Hills Hotel, only to emerge at the other side with a laminated business card, ready to make a deal with someone talking about real estate at the other end.

When I heard that story, I thought to myself "That is someone I want to emulate!"

Silverman's industriousness inspired me to start showing houses to customers by helicopter, and then eventually wrapping houses in big red bows when escrow closed. People don't forget these things and if you can be creative, even if it costs you some extra money, it will pay off at the end of the day. When you close escrow, always do something special for the buyer. Don't just leave a key and a garage clicker for them. Go out of your way to do something exciting that they won't forget. You'll get more than just a sale—you'll get a fantastic recommendation!

Learn How to Price a Property

When Lawrence Block, the first real estate agent in Beverly Hills, would be asked how much a property was worth, he would always respond, "Whatever someone is willing to pay for it."

This statement stands true today, however we have a lot more tools to use than Lawrence Block did when he was selling the first lots in Beverly Hills.

Today, as an agent we look at comparable properties to set values. It does not necessarily mean the house you are trying to sell is worth the same, but it helps. The most important thing you can do for yourself and for your clients is to learn the inventory. Learn every single facet of the inventory and know more than any other agent.

One of the greatest feelings I have is when I impress my buyers or sellers by telling them sales of different properties recently and in years past. It shows that I know what I am talking about and that I am on top of my game. It is also an important part of the job. I need to know this information so I can accurately put a price on a property. Even if I do not have a buyer for a particular property I attend its open house because I want to see what the inventory is, and then when it sells I want to know why that home sold for that price.

175

I cannot stress enough how important this step is. Know the prices, know the stories of why people are selling, know who the sellers are, know as much as you can. For instance, in some cases, there will be a really low sale or a really high sale in a neighborhood. Know why the neighbor's house sold so cheaply. Know that they sold it to a friend who bailed them out of financial trouble at the last minute.

You want to understand exactly why a house sold for more money so you don't sound like an idiot when the owners of a property you want to list ask you why a house no better than their own sold for twice as much as you are telling them their own house is worth. Knowing that the neighbor bought that property and paid a premium can help you save face—and ultimately, commissions.

Visit the Neighbors First

Before you put a house on the market, always visit the neighbors. There is a great chance that the neighbors will want to buy the property and adjoin it onto their property, especially in high -end neighborhoods.

Confidence

I have always been confident. When I was seven or eight years old, I was sitting with my parents at a restaurant in San Francisco, called Stars. As we sat in the restaurant, I noticed a nicely dressed woman, sitting at the table next to ours. I just leaned over the booth and started talking to her and her husband. They thought I was such a cute six-year-old that we (my parents included) be-

176

came friends and whenever we went to San Francisco we visited them at their home in Pacific Heights.

If you are confident, (being charming helps as well) you can talk to anyone. When I was a little boy, I could talk to any adult especially women, because I was confident, and they found it adorable. Some of my friends will remind me of how when I was younger, at Bar Mitzvahs, I would dance with all their mothers.

You must be confident to succeed in this business. A lot of people assume I am arrogant, but they misjudge me. What they perceive as arrogance is really self-confidence. I am not afraid to talk to strangers and I am not afraid to pick up the telephone and speak to someone who has no idea who I am.

On Burning Bridges; Don't!

Don't burn bridges. If there is anything that I regret, it is burning bridges, regardless of whether I was right or wrong. I mentioned earlier that if you lend someone twenty dollars and you never see them again, it is probably a good thing. You don't have to call that person out of principle to remind them what a terrible person they are. Just stay away from them and keep your thoughts to yourself, because one day, that no good person will have the money to buy a house from you and they will remember how respectable you are. They will then hire you o represent them. Take people's characters for what they are, but don't school them. And if someone does something to you, forgive them, believe me, nothing will annoy them more.

Don't Be Lazy

Lazy people don't get anywhere in life. Unless you can make money lying in your bed, you need to get up. There's opportunity everywhere—but you have to grab it before it passes you by.

There's always opportunity in front of people. If I have a real estate deal and I don't know someone, I will ask a friend to make an introduction and offer him or her a great referral fee for his or her efforts. When someone asks me for an introduction, I don't ask for referrals, but I always make sure to give them, as a courtesy. If I can do something to help another person, I'm happy to do it. If you want to thank me, take me out to dinner.

Sometimes, I ask some of my friends who are my own age, and are just graduating from college to make a connection for me and I will give them a referral fee. In my business, a referral can easily be twenty, thirty or forty thousand dollars depending on the deal. Some of my friends take me up on it, while others don't. I have some friends who only care about what they are having for lunch and what club they are going to that evening, instead of doing a tiny bit of work that could make them a ton of money, they lose out. Money doesn't just come to you. Laziness gets you nowhere... effort makes you rich.

Prioritize Your Time

Don't waste your time on stupid prospects that are going to get you nowhere. You can make a lot more money making deals that are real, than deals you think could be huge, but have a very low probability of ever closing.

When I first got into the business, I thought it would be productive to show two story houses to a ninety-year-old. The gentleman, John, who could definitely afford anything he wanted, wanted to see a bunch of houses. I gladly showed them to him. But then after six months of looking at houses with the guy, my grandmother pointed something out to me, which I should have been able to see from the beginning.

"At ninety-years-old," she told me, "it does not matter how much money you have, the only place you are moving to is the cemetery."

John was bored with his life and wanted to look at houses. He was not about to pack up sixty years of his life and start moving to a bigger spread. You can apply this story to just about any deal—if someone isn't going to buy, they're not going to buy, period. Your energy is better spent on people who are ready to move!

Enjoy Your Money, but Spend it Where You Can Make More

My grandfather always used to say to me, "I don't want to die the richest man in the cemetery."

What he meant by this was he wanted to have a good time while he was alive. A lot of people are slaves to making money. I look at so many people in my business that live and breathe selling houses. They make a lot of money, but they have no life whatsoever. Enjoy your career, but don't let it control you. Take the money you earn. Save half of it. Take another quarter and live off it. Take ten percent of what's left and give it to charity, and take the final fifteen percent and do whatever you want to do with it. If you work, you deserve to enjoy your money. I live by these principles...and even though some of my friends make fun of me

179

and call me cheap, these are fundamentally important ways to live a rewarding life.

Here's a typical example. Some of my friends tease me because I hate valet parking, I don't want to spend $15 to park my car. I would rather do it myself. People don't understand that concept. People also don't understand the concept of how I will go and spend ridiculous amounts of money on traveling. I have no problem spending $500 or $1000 on a room in a hotel for just myself, but you better believe I will have a fit if I have to pay for overnight parking in the hotel.

Everyone is entitled to enjoy their money how they please, but you must enjoy it, because you cannot take it with you. As long as you save half of your income every year, you will be a self -made millionaire at a very young age. My grandmother taught me this when I was very young and it is something that is entrenched in my head.

Charity

Before I started making my own money, I could never figure out why my family gave so much money away to charity. I thought it was ridiculous. When I started making my own money, I finally discovered why they were so charitable.

Money isn't forever. You can't take it with you and you can help a lot of other people along the way. Aside from giving money to charity, it's crucial for you to become active in different charities in your community. From a business perspective, it's very productive because you will make a ton of contacts and people will also see that you are not just focused on yourself.

Pick a charity that means something to you, something that can help you for the rest of your life. I focus my time on Jewish charities. By putting your efforts—and your money—towards something that can benefit your community, you get more than contacts—you get kudos, and those go a long way!

Be A Million Dollar Agent

Never be afraid to try something new. Remember, amateurs built the Ark. Professionals built the Titanic.
-- Unknown

You have to be aggressive in life, because no one is going to hand you anything. If you don't want something badly enough, then you don't deserve it. In 2006, Bravo released a show called, Million Dollar Listing. The show is about several agents in Los Angeles trying to move overpriced properties in an inflated market.

After watching the show a few times, I thought to myself "Gee I can do that. Not only do I handle more expensive and more impressive homes than they do, but the clients I deal with and the situations I am involved with are much funnier and more entertaining."

I made some phone calls and I got through to the production company that produced the show, World of Wonder. I actually called them out of the blue. I introduced myself and told them I'd like to interview to be on the next season of the show. Now it is very possible that they would have called me anyhow, but I wasn't going to wait for them. I knew that all I needed was ten minutes in front of the producers to prove to them that I was the right guy for this show.

Ten minutes turned into an hour and one half, and before I knew it, I was the on the television show. That's how it happened, and it may never have if I wasn't ready to pick up the phone and take a chance.

Don't Accept A Lunch Invitation Until You Know Why You Are Meeting

Due to my television appearances, and because my contact information is listed on my website, I get calls on a daily basis from people around the country asking me questions, picking my brain, or telling me they want to buy a house. I would say that if one out of a hundred calls is a legitimate lead, that's lucky. You have to remember how many millions of people have seen me on television and out of those millions of viewers, there are a lot of whack jobs.

When I get a phone call, I first Google the person I am talking to. If I cannot find them, I ask them what I can do for them and if they say they want to meet to discuss business, I ask them specifically what they need. You see, people have opportunities they want to pitch all the time and they figure if they can get in front of you, they have a better shot of earning your business.

If I ask someone what he or she wants to talk about and they say, "I don't really want to get into it on the phone, but I would rather meet in person."

I always say, "No problem, when you are ready to tell me what you're interested in on the phone, call me back."

I am not about to sit down with a stranger. Of course, I say it a little more politely. They usually then give me a sales pitch on a product or something that will better their lives and only waste my time, at which point I say I am not interested.

Just a Couple of Words to Leave you With

I'm a social Democrat, I'm a financial Republican, and I'm pro-choice. I believe anyone has the right to get married be it a man and a woman, a man and a man or a woman to a woman. I'm pro guns. In other words, don't come into my house unannounced or I will show you a whole new meaning of the name, Charlton Heston. I have an unhealthy fascination with my grandmother, I love my parents, I love my boyfriend, and I'm prone to growing moles.

That's the long and short of it. As George Burns would say, "Good Night Gracie."